D0205571

Marketing Long-Term and Senior Care Services

The *Health Marketing Quarterly* series, William J. Winston, Editor:

ABOUT THE EDITOR

William J. Winston is Dean of the School of Health Services Management, Golden Gate University, San Francisco and Managing Associate of the Professional Services Marketing Group, a health marketing consulting firm in San Francisco.

Marketing Long-Term and Senior Care Services

William J. Winston
Editor

The Haworth Press
New York

Marketing Long-Term and Senior Care Services has also been published as *Health Marketing Quarterly,* Volume 1, Number 4, Summer 1984.

The Haworth Press, Inc., 28 East 22 Street, New York, NY 10010

Library of Congress Cataloging in Publication Data
Main entry under title:

Marketing long-term and senior care services.

(The Health marketing quarterly series)
"Has also been published as Health marketing quarterly, volume 1, number 4, summer 1984"—T.p. verso.
Includes bibliographical references.
1. Long-term care of the sick—Marketing—Addresses, essays, lectures. 2. Aged—Medical care—Marketing— Addresses, essays, lectures. I. Winston, William J. II. Health marketing quarterly. III. Series.
RA644.5.M37 1984 362.1'6'0688 84-6716
ISBN 0-86656-289-3

Marketing Long-Term
and Senior Care Services

Health Marketing Quarterly
Volume 1, Number 4

CONTENTS

Preface

In this issue the *Health Marketing Quarterly* is directed towards *Long-Term and Senior Care Services* after the successful issues of *Marketing the Group Practice* and *Marketing for Mental Health Services*. The next two issues will be applied to *Marketing Hospital Services* and *Marketing Ambulatory Care Services.*

EDITORIAL

The editorial topic is about the potential use of telecommunication systems in marketing health and human services. An example of technological influence on marketing services is the use of videotex systems. Health marketers will be required to become more familiar with advanced techniques as the complexity of the health marketplace intensifies. The editorial briefly describes the potential use of videotex systems in marketing health services.

INTRODUCTION TO ARTICLES

Long-term and senior care services have been seriously neglected in applied resources for marketing. In fact, the concept of marketing long-term and senior care services is relatively new. The initial article by Ben Abramovice starts the reader off by explaining the definition and elements of long-term and senior care marketing; elaborating on why marketing is vitally needed for senior services; provides a historical perspective of long-term care; and gives a description of the specific components of a marketing program for long-term and senior care.

The area of senior programs spans more than forty different services and encompasses a complex environment beyond those of the traditional health care field. In the second article, Connie Evashwick describes why a rigorous approach to marketing is needed for new senior services. The article reviews the basic steps in marketing; describes how services for seniors differ from other health services; and outlines examples of specific marketing strategies.

The third article by Joseph B. McCarthy and Lily L. Hurlimann surveys the important changes within the health marketplace which are reinforcing greater amounts of competition. The authors then examine how the increased competition is rapidly changing the role of the health care marketer and the applications of health marketing.

As the long-term and senior care marketplace changes, one of the important applications of marketing is the use of market auditing. In the fourth article, Albert V. Aguiar elaborates on the practical aspects of using marketing research to develop a marketing audit for extended care services.

From the marketing audit information the senior service can identify gaps in the marketplace in which the organization can position itself. In the fifth article, I present the basic strategies for positioning the long-term and senior care services in the community.

A major service area for the maturing population is mental health services. During the last few years mental health services have increased dramatically for senior citizens. Sharon George explores the different market strategies which senior care mental health planners and administrators can utilize and outlines how marketing can reduce the misunderstandings about mental illness in the sixth article.

The seventh article by Matthew Midgett expands on the specific marketing techniques and strategies for a major delivery mechanism within long-term care, the Skilled Nursing Facility.

The need to control and direct marketing expenditures to achieve maximum benefits is an important management function for health and human service administrators. James B. Suver and John A. Miller explain in the eighth article the importance of selecting appropriate objectives in measuring the effectiveness of the marketing program; provide specific examples of marketing programs which developed clearly stated marketing objectives and outputs; and present a cost/revenue modeling approach to marketing control.

An important aspect of marketing is the reasoning about why and how a consumer selects a senior service. In the last article, Scott Smith outlines his research findings on the identification of the decision variables which are important for family decision makers in selecting alternative senior services. This information can provide an excellent base to better understand the behavior of the long-term and senior care consumer and plan for future services.

I hope that administrators and marketers who manage to provide long-term and senior care services will find this issue a helpful resource in communicating to the medical marketplace and community about their worthwhile services.

William J. Winston
Editor

Marketing Long-Term and Senior Care Services

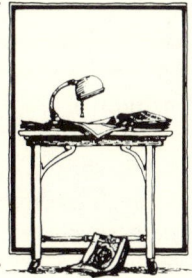

Is the Future of Health Marketing Going to Be Directed by Videotex Systems?

Videotex is an interactive electronic system in which data and graphics are transmitted from a computer network over telephone or cable lines and displayed on a subscriber's TV or computer-terminal screen. According to the American Marketing Association, Sam Fedida, a research engineer for the British Post Office, is credited as the 'father of videotex' during the late 1960s. In 1974 he created a working model of videotex and it was produced commercially in 1979. During the 1970s videotex expanded throughout Europe and Japan. Evidently the first videotex usage occurred in the United States in 1978 by a TV station in Utah.

Videotex is typically provided on a subscription basis by private firms. There are approximately twenty-five private videotex firms in the United States, including AT&T, Chemical Bank and The Dow Jones Co. These videotex firms provide a wide range of services such as: news, sports, financial, at-home banking, travel information, magazines, games, instructional sessions, directories, employ-

1

ment listings, home energy management, electronic mailings, security scanning, and medical monitoring. Consumer companies view videotex as a major channel for advertising and direct-marketing of their products/services. Marketing research firms see the medium as a tremendous channel for consumer auditing or marketing research.

Videotex marketing was not expected to be a major new marketing medium until the 1990s or later. However, the home computer industry has changed the entire framework of the future of marketing. Few people foresaw the current growth in the personal computer marketplace nor did they think personal computers could be easily adapted for videotex viewing. It was also perceived that consumers were going to have to spend considerable sums for videotex terminals if they subscribed. It is now estimated that nearly 20 million households will have home computer systems by 1990, up from approximately four million in 1984. The only major addition which is needed to convert a typical home computer system to a videotex system is a modem. A modem is a communications link by telephone, cable or satellite channels from the home computer to the videotex information firm. Modems are now becoming relatively inexpensive and will be more commonly attached to most computer systems by the turn of the decade. Some innovative companies are already producing videotex conversion devices which are compatible with select home computer systems. Since IBM has become the major producer of personal computers it is probable that most conversion devices will be adaptable to their systems. Standardization should develop quickly for most computer systems by 1990 for videotex. By 1985 it is almost certain that videotex software programs will become available through your local computer store.

The American public is becoming more and more computer literate and accepting of computers into their homes and offices. As this trend continues people will gradually become willing, and possibly anxious, for greater access to business and personal information through their computer systems. However, there will be 'growing pains' for the consumer and the producers of videotex systems. People are very slow to change their habits and develop confidence in new technology. For example, people will have to become used to 'reading' off their monitors or TV screens with only three or four paragraphs visible at any one time. Also publishers are not totally ready to abandon their traditional paper and print procedures.

Despite these basic problems there is considerable optimism for videotex development. The use of videotex marketing and information gathering may change many of our day-to-day activities. The potential for home education, service delivery, and shopping is tremendous. It was projected in 1980 that very few people would ever convert to using bank cards instead of using traditional bank services. It is now expected that over 50% of consumers will use bank cards for their day-to-day banking systems by 1987. I sincerely believe people adapt a lot quicker than they are given credit for by traditional conservative forecasters.

Health and human services suffer from a tremendous gap in communicating with the general public. There still is considerable consumer ignorance about available community services, alternative treatment procedures, self-help strategies, costs of services, comparative insurance plans, and general health education. The potential for videotex systems to help in educating the consumer about health and human services is huge. In addition, the access for improving our marketing research techiques and marketing our services directly to the consumer or provider through videotex has great advantages. For example, hospitals or long-term care facilities could market their services directly to the consumer or improve their knowledge of the psychographic/lifestyle profiles of the population. Medical equipment firms or pharmaceutical companies can educate medical providers as to new innovations or drugs that are available. Insurance companies will be able to explain their health packages directly through terminals to employees or consumers. Contracting related to Preferred Provider Organizations would be accomplished through the videotex system to medical providers or hospitals. Public health agencies will have direct access to the population for prevention education. There are unlimited positive aspects to the future development of videotex systems for marketing health and human services. Within the last decade health administrators have had to become acquainted with computer systems for forecasting, budgeting, billing, medical records, and treatment activities. The personal computer is currently becoming common in small and large health organizations. It will only be a matter of time before we begin to use the communication potential of the computer. The future of improving our marketing techniques will be related to making use of the telecommunication technology that will be upon us in a very short time. All health marketers must become familiar with computer systems and keep abreast of the technological changes that are occurring. It is necessary for the health marketer/administrator to be 'ready' to apply this new technology when it does become available. It is almost certain that videotex systems will become a major marketing and communicating tool of the late 1980s and early 1990s.

William J. Winston
Editor

Marketing Long Term and Senior Care Services

Ben Abramovice

In discussing the issue of marketing of long term care service, we must come to grips with certain realizations about our own administrative practices.

First of all, we must recognize that the concept of marketing in our field is relatively new. As a matter of fact, it's been only in the last few years that marketing in the hospital field has assumed the stature of having specialists act as head of marketing or director of a marketing department. It is not that long ago that many far-thinking academic institutions began to teach health marketing with, of course, the emphasis on the acute hospital. In order for us to begin a serious dialogue on the issue of marketing in long term care, one must accept that marketing is here to stay and that the factors that have created the need for marketing in most of the health fields relate directly to our long term care services.

I have heard on many occasions that people have trouble with the word marketing because of its relationship to the shabbier side of the corporate world, to advertising agencies that have very low degrees of credibility, and to shabby practices in retail trade. Maybe what we're talking about is the need to utilize a different word to sooth our sensitivities. Regardless of what word we call the action, the process of marketing has a significant role in the successful functioning of all long term care facilities and services.

To carry these introductory comments on marketing one step further, we must also acknowledge that there is a wide diversity in the long term care field, and that certain elements within long term care are already on the path of developing very sophisticated marketing approaches. This will lead us into a much more specific discussion of long term care and its varied elements.

Ben Abramovice, Executive Director, Laguna Honda Hospital, San Francisco, CA (Note—largest long-term care facility in the United States); Adjunct Professor in Long-Term Care Administration, Golden Gate University, San Francisco, CA.

DEFINITION OF MARKETING

We should recognize that in non-profit circles the term marketing has certain negative connotations. It is linked with "Madison Avenue" advertising and some of the less desirable parts of the retail trade business. We've also already recognized that marketing as a specialty field is relatively new in the health field in general, and it is still having difficulty being accepted as part of the acute hospital modus operandi. Needless to say, whatever we have learned about marketing in the health field has come from our experiences in the acute hospital, and that in itself must point to the need to modify practices to suit the long term care.

We must recognize that long term care is considerably different than the acute hospital field, and therefore, while certain basic techniques might be applicable, possibly definitions and processes may be quite different. One way to define marketing is as a way of doing business or a way of thinking about management. Some have even called it management philosophy. It is important to spend some time in pursuing this definition of marketing because it may be necessary to custom tailor this definition to suit the long term care field.

We would have to agree that the long term care delivery unit, whether it be a nursing home, residential care facility, or adult day health, has a service that it wishes to deliver to some component of the community. The second realization that we must accept is that in order to make this linkage we have to describe the service in the most optimal manner possible to suit the perceived needs of the people that would use the service. The next most logical component of this definition is that we should be very, very clear on who the individuals or groups are that would benefit from the use of this service. We must be very specific in defining that group, and we must be very direct in bringing the description of our services to that group in the most appropriate and successful manner.

This attempt at definition of marketing falls short in that it is a brief synopsis of the marketing process. If one were to accept the premise that marketing is a component of management that assures the appropriate match between the service and the user of the service, and that this broad view allows the process to go on indefinitely, one can incorporate marketing as a bonafide philosophy of management. Once marketing is accepted at this level and incorporated as part of management activity on a routine basis, then the definition of marketing is complete. If we look, however, at marketing as a project that must take place at only certain periods of time, it ceases to become defined as management philosophy and assumes a much less significant role in the efforts of any organization to render its service successfully to a defined community. In other words, this definition of marketing is: the effort of bringing your services, which are presumably the right services to the right user at the right time, at the right place, at the right price; and that if this is your intention as an organization, marketing must be an ongoing function. So by description we have defined what marketing is in long term care.

In order to place marketing at the proper level in management process, one must note the difference between marketing, advertising, promotion and public relations. If one were to accept marketing as the "umbrella" philosophy, then these other terms would easily fit as sub-components to the broad marketing philosophy that management could choose to adhere to.

While we must remember that marketing *is not and should not be an attempt to force customers to accept a service they don't need,* it may be necessary to define in the marketing approach, goods or services that may or should be needed by the potential customer. Once you cross the line, however, and attempt through marketing methods to coerce the acquisition of the goods or services by a customer, you have, in essence, crossed the line into that area of marketing that has caused great public disfavor. You should recognize that you are entering an area that *no longer is appropriate,* in my opinion, in terms of ethical conduct for the long term care field. Unfortunately, there are elements within the health system that have chosen this most negative of the "Madison Avenue" approaches to selling their services, and as a result the legitimacy of the concepts of marketing are constantly being challenged.

MARKETING PROGRAM

Before we involve ourselves with specific marketing approaches that relate to different elements within the continuum of care, I wish to discuss, in a somewhat academic way, the elements of marketing, and then move on to how this basic format can be utilized for your particular organization. A knowledge of the history of long term care and of the continuum is necessary to understand where service fits into the entire scheme. If you do not understand this you will not be able to perfect a marketing plan that's appropriate for the long term care client. You will always be out of synch with the reality of the total system, and run into the hazards of "missing the boat" because you don't understand the relationship of the continuum or the historical prospective to the delivery and acceptance of your service.

Having just defined marketing, I think it appropriate that we take some time to define long term care. For the sake of this particular article, we will relate to long term care only in the context of its services to the elderly population. I acknowledge that approximately 5% of the institutional beds relate to non-elderly people who use long term care services. This 5% consists of developmentally disabled, cerebral palsy, mentally retarded, mentally ill and an array of other handicaps including long term trauma, chronic pediatric birth defects, etc. Because these particular areas require long term care which is highly specific to the particular ailment involved, they should be addressed at another time.

Suffice to say, discussing this topic in relationship to the aging population is a large enough endeavor.

Another aspect of long term care that should be recognized is that 60-70% of elderly people are supported by family, neighborhood church, or other aspects of an informal network, and may not be perceived as needing long term care services. As we move along in our discussion, however, we will see that this may not be so. A final caveat is that I am using 65 or older as a definition of elderly, even though HUD may use 55 and Social Security may use 62 and many statistical studies use 60. This unfortunate ambiguity in defining elderly will nag us indefinitely, and is a great deterrent to formulation of good public policy and good service delivery strategy. Nevertheless, it will help in picking the most commonly used definitions of the group we are addressing.

HISTORICAL PERSPECTIVE OF LONG TERM CARE

Let's put things in order. Long term care as we know it has its origin—at least in Western, industrialized society—with the English Poor Laws. Let us pick a starting point, say for example, Dickensonian England, where elderly disabled and mentally ill were removed from public sight and placed in almshouses. The almshouse or poor house, sponsored either by a church or a rich benefactor, were the origins of the institutional framework that set the stage for the development of institutional care in the United States. The concept of local government caring for the elderly in the form of county farms and almshouses spread so that it was the predominant form of care up through the 1900s in the United States. Additionally, the nonprofit, charitable and fraternal organizations—church groups, the Masons, Oddfellows, and a variety of other "fraternal groups" encouraged the building of facilities to care for the members of their group. There was no significant change in this pattern of a loosely, non-affiliated group of institutions through the '30s.

In the mid-30s, when the full impact of the depression created a very visible impoverished elderly group, the government chose to single out and financially support elderly needs in laws that were passed in 1935. At this time there was no significant, visible profit-making component. There were, as there had been in the past, sanitaria to care for wealthy people, but by and large they were not very numerous and had very low visibility. There was no significant linkage between those facilities housing elderly, disabled, and mentally ill and the hospital field per se.

After World War II the whole medical care system made a quantum leap forward. This was due to the technology explosion, which included antibiotics, special surgical techniques, and a totally new rehabilitation field. We note that going into the '50s there emerged a rest home or nursing home that had an affiliation with an acute hospital, usually at the end of what was called progressive patient care. All through the '50s the problems of the emerging elderly population became more apparent so that by the late '50s and early '60s, care of the elderly was a major socio-political issue. The first White House Conference on Aging which was called in 1961, supported the creation of Medicare, Medicaid laws and encouraged the rapid increase in nursing home beds throughout the country. Incorporated in the reimbursement formula at that time, were incentives to attract private capital. This was a reflection of the government policy at the time. The creation of a profit-making nursing home industry was challenged by the recognition that in order to serve the elderly population properly and assure that people were not placed inappropriately in an institutional setting, a broader continuum of services were needed. Consequently, during the early '70s, the concept of the continuum of care gained a great deal of support. This continuum seems to be the primary conceptual base for the evolution of long term care in the future. The continuum itself is a unique service matrix designed to give the appropriate service at the appropriate time in an effort to keep the elderly person independent and physically and socially functioning as long as possible. Until the successful development of the continuum takes place, the predominant characteristic of this long term care system is the institution.

THE CONTINUUM OF CARE

As I mentioned, the continuum of care was a concept that evolved during the early '70s and now appears to be pointing the way towards evolution of long term care for the '80s. In my description, the continuum includes both institutional and non-institutional services. To be more on target, we must remember that the minority of elderly will be involved in the long term care as it is currently construed. That is primarily because the long term care continuum is conceived as being useful only to those people who have health needs. My own definition of the long term continuum deals with people who are relatively healthy. This approach diverges considerably from contemporary health mode or medical model of the continuum.

Let us start, however, with this medical model of continuum that starts with people who are in need of services which may not be specifically classified as health services. Also, for the sake of discussion, let us assume that we start with the elderly person in their home. This can be either a house or apartment, a granny cottage, some space in their children's home; or even a downtown hotel. As a regressive cycle begins to set in they need a more protective environment. The next step in this brick and mortar continuum, which unfortunately emphasizes the regressive component of aging, would be senior housing. Sometimes known as 202 projects, 236 projects, sometimes funded by nonprofit groups. In these kinds of settings a more protective environment can be designed, and often an array of support services such as meals, housekeeping, and health oriented services can be delivered to the person in their own apartment.

At some point in the future, for those that regress, their need is to go into a residential care facility. This offers room and board, 24 hour awake support, assistance with medication, some social component and a variety of other non-medical services. If a person continues to regress, the residential care home (also known as a boarding home for the aged or rest home) will no longer be satisfactory. At this time the individual must move into the health field, and hopefully into an intermediate care facility. This best may be described as a skilled nursing facility staffed at about 80% of the manpower, and offering reimbursement rate of approximately 80% of the skilled nursing reimbursement.

The skilled nursing facility, otherwise known as a convalescent hospital or nursing home, is the next step in the continuum. And then the final step will be the acute hospital.

This is only the brick and mortar part of the continuum. What really makes the continuum work are those services that are designed to prevent regression and enable an elderly person to stay independent longer.

The first sub-system is the outreach system, which may originate free standing or at an institution, but which is designed to bring a variety of services into the home of the elderly person. These services, such as Meals on Wheels, Home Health Aide, Choreworker, Visiting Nurse, etc., may be brought in to any of the brick and mortar facilities. They can be brought directly to the person's home. They can go to a residential care facility. Some of them can even go to the nursing homes.

The second component of this continuum is a sub-system that we will call the senior center. Here a variety of services are offered, such as nutrition, health, paramedical clinic, legal counseling, etc. People are transported to the system to receive services. Here again, the goal is to keep people as independent as long as possible. The main factor in the senior center concept, is, of course, transportation. It is altogether possible that the outreach system and the senior center system can be part of the same entity.

The third and most significant component to the continuum of care is the informal network, comprised of neighbors, families, churches, and so on. This may be combined with the outreach system or senior center.

What this shows us is that not only are all of the services in the continuum directed towards maintaining the independence of the individual, but that the regressive path as represented by the brick and mortar continuum is counteracted by the supportive action of the outreach center and informal systems.

If one were to go even further, one would find a specific agency for each one of these services that are delivered to the elderly. In order for us to be thorough in our exploration of the marketing for long term care, we must therefore go into a thorough analysis of the elements of marketing. Let us define a marketing program in five major steps.

1. Organizational "buy-in"
2. User Needs Analysis
3. Marketing Plan
4. Marketing Communication
5. Evaluation and Change

ORGANIZATIONAL BUY-IN

The most important and leading component of the marketing program is the organizational "buy-in". I am using this phraseology to indicate that the decision making component of the organization, whether it's the administration, the ownership or a non-profit board of directors, must, after careful analysis of the circumstances and need for marketing, accept a marketing program as a major organizational philosophy. If there is no organizational "buy-in", the other aspects of the marketing program will not be effectively implemented.

Sometimes, in order to get involved with the organizational "buy-in", a presentation by an outside professional through the office of the administrator may be necessary. There may be a need for a tremendous selling job describing all of the ramifications of the marketing program to the board of directors or the ownership. (Or until the administration actually says, "Yes, we want a marketing program.")

There are many deterrents to this organizational "buy-in". One of them is the fact that many long term care facilities find that their services are in demand and that this "fat cat" status, i.e., with a waiting list for their services, causes them to wonder at the need for marketing. What must be pointed out is how quickly the marketplace changes. There are many examples of organizations that find themselves with waiting lists one day, and because of organizational or demographic changes, with low census or low utilization of services the next day.

In these cases, the marketing plan must be presented as a way to hedge against the future and protect the organization from being hit by some unknown downside risk that is hidden in the marketplace. But let's not deal too much longer with the "fat cats" who have tremendous demand for their services. Let us assume that they will be wise enough to recognize the risk inherent in complacency. Let's deal with those services that must be presented to a consumer in a competitive marketplace. Let us assume that it is important for the service to sell itself in order for it to be utilized and that the demand for it may or may not be there. Let's accept also, that there is no overwhelming utilization of this service.

It is this type of organization, where the "buy-in" has the most significance. There may still be a need for an outside individual, a specialist in marketing, to present this for acceptance by the board or ownership.

USER NEEDS ANALYSIS

After the organizational buy-in, the next most important step is to analyze the needs of the potential users of services. In the case of long term care which is a marketplace of elderly people, research must take place that will help pinpoint what the elderly need or want. Whether you start out determining the need to build a nursing home, or start a senior nutrition site, an in depth analysis of the potential customers of this service must be made. Although it may seem crass to call the elderly who use the service "customers", from the standpoint of marketing, they are people who will purchase goods and services.

One aspect of analyzing the marketplace for the elderly is to know about existing resources that have done needs analysis of the elderly population in a particular area. One resource, of course, is your Area Agency on Aging (AAA). The second is the existing local planning agency. Very often, the state department on aging or various advocate groups in the area have done their own needs analysis, and with a high degree of accuracy, can pinpoint the potential market in that particular aging community.

Additionally, there are many government publications including the White House Conference documentation, and information from the National Institute on Aging that can give you broad directions and trends that may be taking place in the marketplace. Research papers that examine the personal characteristics, habits, shopping behavior, and leisure time activities of consumers have been published in well known professional journals.

To analyze the marketplace for nursing home beds, for example, one would research out the bed quotas through the local health planning agency. A discussion with discharge planners will tell you very quickly about the demand for beds. The same process would assist you in determining the need for residential care beds. Let us assume that you have analyzed the marketplace, and determined that there is a need for a service you are currently delivering. You now want to assure yourself of a continuing, steady flow of business. This means that your marketing plan must, as we have discussed in the past, be on an ongoing program, one that keeps you in touch with the particular market of users for your service.

A most important point is that you will need very specific data. For example, it is very important to know the discharge pattern of your local hospitals to determine the referral pattern and potential attrition into your facility. It is very important to understand the nature of the continuum of care, so that you can project the potential users of residential care based on the marketplace for senior housing and seniors living in their homes. It is necessary to determine the specific number of people who are unable to leave their home for meals. This will allow you to determine if your own home meal program will have enough business to be viable. The specificity in terms of numbers of users, their geographic dispersal, and their economic capability must be done in as an exact manner as possible.

The analysis of the user market may take a significant investment and it may be worth it. It is one thing to analyze a market for a particular service that needs only flexible resources, such as additional units of personnel; it is another thing to analyze a market that will require millions of dollars worth of capital investment. Point in fact, if this is the case, and millions of dollars of capital investment is going to be required, it is to your decided advantage to have the marketplace analyzed professionally. The high degree of accuracy that a professional market feasibility can provide you, may save many improperly invested dollars, may redirect your development, or may even encourage you to cancel the project entirely.

MARKETING PLAN

The marketing plan is nothing more than a series of decisions set on a certain time scale, that will ultimately reach a certain goal. The goal in this case is the acquisition of your service by the customer or consumer. This plan will take the data received by the user research, move into the development phase so that the service is created by your organization, communicate the existence of this service to the market, and then evaluate the reception of this service by the marketplace. This plan, sometimes called the strategic plan, is worth a great deal of your time and effort, because if it is successful, you and your organization will be successful also.

MARKETING COMMUNICATION

At first blush the elements of marketing communication may appear to be very familiar. In organizational life, we have all experienced the need to produce a brochure or some descriptive literature about our service. Most likely you have gone through the process of evaluating a variety of kinds of advertisements that would be put in either the yellow pages or pieces of literature that are circulated throughout the community. Few administrative people have not been involved in some kind of marketing communication. Most of the time, however, we called it public relations and attribute other motives to this particular action. One aspect of this generic form of communication is that it probably is a public relations vehicle and should be considered as such. Not that marketing is qualitatively different from public relations at every interface; it's that public relations and marketing should be viewed as different processes to deal with different managerial philosophies. That's not to say that a particular piece of literature or action would not be both a public relations vehicle and a marketing vehicle.

Let us say, however, that we have a communication in mind that recognizes a marketing approach that requires a great deal of analysis, both from the standpoint of the specific public to be reached and the specific definition of the product or service to present to them. We then must design a communication vehicle that has as much technological analysis, targeting, and design that we can build into it.

Let us outline a few of the most common, and I may add reliable communication devices.

A. *Personal Communication*

In my experience, one of the most successful means of marketing communication is the individual approach, which says that you as an administrator or an appropriate member of your organization must make direct contact with the population to be marketed. If you have pinpointed a specific elderly group, or if your marketing target is for example for discharge planners or physicians, nothing is better than a very positive, well-constructed, personal appearance.

If you are in the process of marketing your nursing home, few things can beat your meeting the physician that will ultimately refer a patient to you. If you rely heavily on discharge planners, your personal contact with them is very important; let them see you and the quality of management you represent. The presumption is that you have the instrinsic capability to do these presentations. Do not overestimate your capability; if you are strong in many aspects of management, but not in this one, do not do yourself a disservice; use someone else in your organization who is better able to appeal on a personal level. The ability to communicate to individuals or groups and market directly in this fashion usually will lead to successful accomplishment of your marketing goals. To some degree, it offers you speedy feedback as to the success of your ability or to the positive reception of your communication.

Usually, however, it is best to carry with you certain written materials to leave with the people you have spoken to.

B. Printed Material

The development of pamphlets, brochures and other written promotional material is an art form unto itself. The quality, style and design vary widely, depending on the amount of money you're putting into it, the image you want to portray, and the kind of technical assistance you use in developing it. It is important that an individual who uses the personal communication vehicle, use written literature to leave or distribute. There are many professional people who can assist you in designing literature about your service. Your best approach, of course, is to get pieces of literature that can be both hand carried and delivered through the mail. Very often, pieces of distributable literature will have components allowing the user of the service to respond back to you either in a request for further information, or in response to certain questions posed in the literature. In any event, one or more pieces of printed material are imperative in virtually any marketing program.

C. Media Communications

Developing part of your marketing program using media such as radio, TV, or the newspapers, is considered by many to be a cost effective approach. The drawbacks are your lack of ability to do target marketing, and the assumption that the general public who will read or hear or see this form of communication will be self-selective. Both television and radio have free public service announcements (PSA), which should not be overlooked by nonprofit organizations. Most organizations are able to make a list of named individuals in radio and television stations as well as the key person in your newspapers who will handle news releases and public service announcements. If you are unfamiliar with how to write a public service announcement or tape one, a brief meeting with any of the PSA directors in your local tv or radio stations will clear this up very quickly. There are also many professionals in the field who can assist you in making PSAs.

In terms of using the "mass" media for marketing communication, we must recognize that there is a substantial expense, and a very difficult time monitoring the return. Paid advertising in newspapers, tv and radio are perceived are to be very efficient and acceptable marketing approaches.

The yellow pages of your telephone directory are a must for any of the services that you will be selling. Believe it or not, people will go to the telephone book before they will approach information and referral agencies and other more sophisticated approaches to routing individuals into your service system.

D. Group Events

To some extent this approach is related to the personal communication.

In essence you are inviting a group to an event that could be a talk, a discussion, a multi-media presentation, a contest such as a raffle.

When planning the "event" approach to marketing, you must: 1) include developed, selected guest lists, 2) manage the logistics, 3) plan the presentations that will be made and 4) find some way to assess the success of the event.

EVALUATION AND CHANGE

The most overlooked component of marketing plan is that which evaluates the effectiveness of your program. Monitoring the purchase or acquisition of the services you are offering is important. You find a way to analyze the reception in the marketplace in such a manner that corrective action can be taken on at least two levels. First of all, you want to find out from your evaluation process whether the product or service you are marketing has merit, and meets the needs of the consumer. The second component of your evaluation is the determination of how successful your marketing plan is: that is has your communication been successful, did you analyze the consumer market adequately, did you design and package your service appropriately?

An otherwise successful service delivery system fails because they don't know what went wrong. It could be any one of a number of things, including misdirected mail, improper demographic data, wrong analysis of consumer economics. Very often, the analysis of a marketing program allowing you to change "midstream" may be the only thing that will save an otherwise good project. Your evaluation may also indicate that you should scrub the whole program, thus enabling you to cut your losses.

The quality of life led by the elderly who have health problems can be greatly enhanced by their receiving appropriate services at the right time.

The ability of service providers to understand this dynamic and respond accordingly can be greatly enhanced by adopting a management philosophy that incorporates professional, ethical and effective marketing programs.

Marketing Services for Seniors

Connie Evashwick, Sc.D.

. . . A hospital in Florida built a life care community, expecting to be flooded with applications from seniors desiring security and sun. After 5 years, the life care community still has unsold units, and the hospital has lost millions of dollars and suffered a decrease in its bond rating. In contrast, in Wisconsin, a senior housing project has expanded into nursing home care and supervised living, and saved the hospital from financial disaster.

. . . In the South, a hospital started a geriatric assessment team at the request of the state and is being paid to evaluate and refer Medicaid patients. The hospital has gained an unexpected source of revenue. The physicians have accepted the assessment program and begun to refer their own patients. Patients are receiving more appropriate care; the state is spending less on nursing home care. In Illinois, a geriatric assessment program initiated by a hospital with grant funds has not been accepted by the physicians, and thus lacks regular referrals. Consequently, it has developed no permanent base for patients and has not attained financial solvency. It is likely to cease when the grant funds stop.

. . . A day care program in Washington has closed because it was unable to attract enough patients, despite the fact that there were only two other day care programs in the entire metropolitan area. Meanwhile, a day care program in California has become self-supporting during its first year of operations and now forms the base for an expanded geriatric care program.

What determines the difference between the successful and unsuccessful programs? Those that have flourished have been developed through a rigorous marketing approach. Those that have failed have ignored the basic principles of marketing.

Marketing is defined as: "Analysis, planning, implementation and control of carefully formulated programs designed to bring

Connie Evashwick is Director of Long-Term Care, Pacific Health Resources, Inc., 1423 South Grand Avenue, Los Angeles, CA 90015.

about voluntary exchanges of values with target markets for the purpose of achieving organizational objectives. It relies heavily on designing the organization offerings in terms of the target markets' needs and desires, and on using effective pricing, communication and distribution to inform, motivate and service the market."[1]

Senior citizens, whose health care needs require a comprehensive, continuing mode of care, offer a significant market for health care organizations. However, the typical approach taken by health care organizations in developing new programs—which is to start a service, assume that it will be used, and ignore market realities—may result in abysmal failure. The purpose of this article is to apply the basic steps of marketing to the initiation of new services for seniors. The basic components of marketing are outlined below. The special considerations required for application to the senior population are highlighted.

RATIONALE: AGING POPULATION AND ENVIRONMENTAL PRESSURES

Senior citizens are becoming a strong market force. The "greying of America" is well recognized. The population over the age of 64 will increase from 22.5 million in 1980 to almost 50 million in 2030.[2] During the same period of time, the percent of the U.S. population which is over the age of 65 will increase from 11 percent to 18-20 percent.[3] Industry is beginning to recognize the power of the senior citizen. The "Pepsi Generation" now includes grey-haired grandfathers; Levi Strauss offers "Levis for men"; *Newsweek* has featured a leotard-clad grandmother as a cover girl.[4] Seniors themselves are attempting to draw attention to both the magnitude of the market and their special needs. For example, a coalition of national aging organizations has recently produced a booklet entitled, "Newer Market—Older People."[5]

Seniors are a natural market for health care institutions. People over the age of 65 are admitted to the hospital three times more frequently than those under the age of 65,[6] and they use more than five times as many bed days per year.[7] About one in five older adults is admitted to the hospital each year.[8] Older people average more than 6.3 visits per person per year to a physician, compared to 4.7 visits per person per year for younger adults.[9] From the perspective of health care organizations, the impact of the senior market is tremendous. People over the age of 65 account for an average of 38 percent of hospital inpatient days,[10] with some hospitals having as high as 60 percent of their bed days filled by seniors. Seniors fill 89 percent of nursing home beds;[11] and 90 percent of home health agency visits are to seniors.[12] Health is one of the primary concerns of older adults. In national and local surveys, health consistently ranks as the second or third most important concern of senior citizens, following only income and personal security.[13]

Health care needs of older people are different from those of younger adults. The problems of seniors tend to be multi-faceted, chronic, and multiple. To be effective, care should be interdisciplinary, continuing over time, and integrating and accessing an array of health, mental health and social services. The health care goals should not necessarily focus on cure, but rather should be to help seniors maintain functional independence. As health care institutions seek to meet environmental pressures through product diversification and vertical integration, serving the senior population is potentially a good fit.

In brief, it would seem that services for seniors would be a natural for health care institutions. What is found, however, is that many health care organizations are jumping in and without appropriate consideration of the complexities of the field. In doing so, they are missing the market. Table 1 compares the characteristics of an emergency room service with those of a "geriatric" service and gives an indication of the relative complexity of embarking into the arena of geriatric services. For years, health care organizations have been accustomed to producing a good product and assuming that it would be used. With medical care, particularly high technology care, this has been feasible because doctors, not consumers, controlled demand. Financial viability has been secondary to contributions to patient care quality and physicians' needs. As health care organizations branch into new services, different principles apply. Hence, the need for rigorous marketing is essential.

STEPS IN MARKETING

STEP ONE: Define Organizational Goals

Health care organizations are becoming involved in services for seniors for a variety of reasons. Hospitals, for example, have started senior programs in order to fill empty beds, to empty filled beds, to generate additional revenues, to offset overhead, to capture new

TABLE 1

Comparison of an "Emergency Room Service" and "Geriatric Services":
Well-Defined versus Great Variation and Undefined

	Emergency Room	Geriatric Services
Service Definition	Well-defined: Levels I, II, III, IV	40+ services; many not well specified
Target Population	People of all ages; victims of accidents, acute episodes of illness	People 60 and older; each service has different market
Competition	Other hospitals; urgi centers	Many health, social service and community agencies
Regulations	State licensure; CON	Federal: Titles XVIII, XIX, XX, Older Americans Act; State: Planning, Health Dept., Welfare Dept.; Local: varies for each service
Accreditation	JCAH detailed specifications	JCAH for SNF, hospital-based home care, hospice. Varied other trade association review. No comprehensive accrediting body
Staffing	M.D., R.N., well-defined patterns	Varies. For many services, not well defined. Should be multi and inter-disciplinary for all services
Space and Equipment	Well-defined	Varies from total facility to no space
Payment	Set fee per visit; third-party reimbursement well-defined	Charges vary; reimbursement varies. For many services, private pay

TABLE 1 (CONT'D)

	Emergency Room	Geriatric Services
Promotion	To ambulance services, fire departments, physicians	To seniors and families

markets, to enhance their community image, to respond to voids in service, and to improve quality of care. To conduct a marketing initiative which is ultimately "successful," the health care organization must decide *why* it wants to explore a new arena of services. The organizational objectives, both programmatic and financial, must be clearly specified and accepted. Because many services for seniors are social or support services, institutions must acknowledge an expansion of the health care organization's traditional role. Moreover, many senior services individually are not highly lucrative; thus the financial realities must be examined in detail and matched with the organizational objectives.

STEP TWO: *Analyze the Market Structure*

Assess the Demand: Once an institution acknowledges the potential for geriatric services and decides to enter this field, a thorough analysis must be made of the demand for specific services. There are many options: more than 40 services, used exclusively or primarily, by seniors, have been identified.[14] These services vary in terms of the patient population served, financing, the physician and staff resources required, state and federal regulatory requirements, and the number of patients optimally served. This wide range of alternatives makes careful marketing all the more important. Table 2 identifies a few of the major services and their pertinent characteristics and demonstrates the range of opportunities, as well as the wide variation among services. Unlike other health care services for which physicians control the demand and use is predictable according to the existence of specific conditions, need and effective demand for senior services is dependent upon consumer choice, third-party reimbursement policies, local availability, transportation, and other environmental factors.

As part of a needs assessment, seniors themselves should be asked about the types of services that they would want to have available,

TABLE 2

Comparison of Characteristics of Select Geriatric Services

	Skilled Nursing Home	Home Health	Day Care	Geriatric Assessment	Health Promotion	Senior Housing
Target Population	Very ill	Short-Term Recovery	Short or Long-Term	Complicated but Undiagnosed Problem	Well	Well
Functional Status	Dependent	Home-Bound	Dependent	Dependent or Independent	Independent	Independent
Major Problem	Physical, Mental	Primary Physical	Physical, Mental, Rehab.	Physical, Mental, Social	None	Security
Staffing	Nursing	Nursing, Soc. Work, Rehab. Therapies	Nursing, Rehab., Soc. Work	Interdisciplinary Team	Health Educators	Manager Only
Space	SNF Facility	Office Only	Large Room, Minimal Equipment	Clinic, Lab	Meeting room, Exercise Room	Residential Complex
Ordinary Operating Hours	24 Hrs/Day	8-10 Hrs/Day	8-10 Hrs/Day	1-2 Clinics/Week	Daily or Weekly Meetings	24 Hrs/Day
Payment	Medicare, Private	Medicare	State Private	Private	Private	Private or HUD

including ones for which they would be willing to pay directly. Unlike health services ordered by physicians, the arena of senior services includes many social and support services selected directly by the consumer, and the potential users may thus be the best indicator of demand. Seniors' perceptions of the need for services, their preferences and their satisfaction with current services should each be examined. Moreover, involvement in the needs assessment stage may help ensure subsequent use of the service. If the developers of the life care community in Florida had consulted with the seniors in the area, they would have known in advance that the market was limited due to the geographical constraints of the proposed facility. Within a health care organization, the social workers, discharge planners, and rehabilitation therapists, as well as the physicians and nurses, may have invaluable insights about the availability of services which would facilitate the maintenance of independence of the senior citizens.

Analyze and Segment the Consumer Market: The senior population cannot be treated as a homogeneous cohort. Those over the age of 65 exhibit as much, if not more, diversity than adults of younger age groups. For example, the vast majority of all persons over the age of 65 have at least one chronic condition.[15] About 17 percent have some type of functional disability so severe that it inhibits the performance of basic activities of daily living;[16] the other 82 percent may have a chronic problem but with varying degrees and types of impairment interfering with daily functioning. Seniors vary in dimensions other than health status. In 1978, 14 percent of those over the age of 65 were below the poverty line, which was just slightly higher than the percent of the total U.S. population below the poverty line.[17] At the same time, about 22 percent of those age 65 and older had incomes of above $15,000 per year.[18] Seniors spend more for both nursing home care and recreational vehicles than adults in any other cohort. Characteristics which are particularly relevant to services potentially offered by health care organizations include health conditions, functional health status, economic status, social support system, housing environment and access to transportation.

Because services for seniors vary considerably in the type of patient they are designed to serve, structure, and reimbursement, it is imperative that a health care organization know to whom it is marketing a potential service. In the initial assessment, an analysis should be made of both the current target population of seniors and the potential population of seniors. Projecting the ultimate use of a service on the total senior population of an existing catchment area can be a financially fatal flaw; yet, this is done all too often.

Evaluate the Competition: A plethora of services for the aged abound in most communities. Before entering a new arena of services for seniors, the health care institution must analyze its competition. It is likely to find far more potential competitors than expected. Home care, for example, may be provided or sponsored by multi-purpose senior centers, church groups, community social groups, the public health department, the public welfare department, the Area Agency on Aging, as well as by proprietary and not-for-profit home health agencies, nursing homes, other hospitals, mental health programs, and community service agencies.

Before taking on such competition, the health care organization must be assured that it has a competitive advantage, such as a guaranteed referral source or the ability to provide a better or less expensive service. In addition, the politics of the local environment must be considered. A clinic or hospital which has worked with a local Visiting Nurses Association for the past twenty-five years may have the resources to start its own home health service. However, the result might create such ill will in the community that the additional revenues may not be worth the high cost to its image, the alienation of local physicians, and the wrath of community agencies and consumers.

Assess the Potential for Collaboration: Many health services administrators are unaware of the existence of the "aging network." Yet, this network can be an invaluable source of information and assistance in implementing new programs for seniors. The Area Agencies on Aging, or "Triple As" or "AAAs," were legislatively created by the 1965 Older Americans Act. There are currently more than 500 AAAs which cover all of the United States. The AAAs are responsible for distributing limited state and federal funds for programs created by the 1965 Older Americans Act, as well as acting as a coordinating and information agency for the many public and private organizations and groups serving the senior community.

Many of the agencies servicing the aged focus on social services and tend to be minimally funded. These represent excellent opportunities for health care organizations to initiate a collaborative venture. The health care organization can contribute resources and the revenue base, while gaining the advantages of agencies competent in social services which already relate to a large number of seniors.

Moreover, a health care organization entering the senior services field can benefit immensely from the publicity and good will offered by having the support of the local aging network. Meal programs are one example of collaboration. A hospital or nursing home may invite the members of a nearby senior center to use its cafeteria, particularly if senior meals can be provided during the hours before or after the staff rush, thus maximizing use of otherwise empty space. In exchange, the senior center may allocate part of its funds for nutrition programs or meals on wheels to the patients of the hospital.

Consider the Regulatory Environment: Federal and state regulations apply differently to the various potential senior services. Regulations in addition to those governing traditional health care programs must be examined. In some states, for example, adult day care must be licensed; in other states there are no regulations governing day care. Home health agencies must get a certificate of need in Florida; in other states home health is governed only by licensing requirements. The regulatory climate is important for senior services, as with any other type of service that the health care organization may initiate, because the regulations will affect both the resources required to start and operate the program and the potential financial success.

Financial Climate: The tremendous upheavals in health care financing also apply to services for seniors. The change in Medicare to case-based payment for inpatient care, which began October 1, 1983, has had a major effect. Similar dramatic changes may be anticipated in the near future. For example, discussions are under way about paying for nursing home care based on the diagnostic related group payment system. California has recently entered into a contract for the provision of care to the Medi-Cal population, which includes many seniors. New regulations make hospice care reimbursed by Medicare on a per case basis, while home care remains paid on a per visit basis. In assessing the financial feasibility of any potential new service, but particularly services for those age 65 or older, portending changes in the financial environment must be considered.

STEP THREE: Product Determination and Definition

Because of the range of potential opportunities in the senior services arena, much of the prior analysis of the market may be done in general terms or examining several alternative services. Eventually, each individual service must be assessed for its contribution to the health care organization's goals for complementary programs and financial viability. One health care system in Southern California recognizes dual criteria. For a program to be initiated, it must meet one of two requirements: the service either breaks even and contributes to the continuum of care as a complement to other existing services, or, it must be financially lucrative and thus able to support the development of other services.

In evaluating the market potential of a new service, the S-curve representing the life cycle of a service may be useful.[19] During the past 15 years, the increased attention to the older population and the availability of funds from public programs has resulted in the creation of many new services. In addition, many long-standing services have been reoriented to have greater focus on the needs of older people. Rapid growth in the understanding of the aging process and the care of older patients is also producing new technologies and modalities of treatment. Placing each of the potential services on the S-curve schematic gives some indication on the relative potential of each service. Geriatric assessment teams, for example, are relatively new and few in number and can be expected to increase. They are at the beginning of the S-curve. Home health programs, which have been in existence for years, are suddenly proliferating in number. They might be placed in the middle of the S-curve. Nursing homes are on the plateau phase of the S-curve in many places because of certificate of need requirements that prohibit the expansion or construction of facilities. Analysis of a new service according to its S-curve stage contributes to determining the potential growth and the state of the art affecting development.

The 2 × 2 table is often used to summarize and compare the potential of services. There are those which are low risk and low potential growth; low risk and high growth; high risk and low growth; and high risk and high growth. Services for seniors fall into each of these categories. Optimally, the health care organization would elect a low risk service and, depending on its goals, a high growth one.

As with any other new program, once the health care organization has decided to initiate a new service, it must be clearly defined. Providers and consumers must know what the service is, for whom it is intended, how to access the service, what the cost is, and what the expected payment sources are. To exert its competitive advantage, the health organization must be specific about how its service differs from other similar services available in the community.

STEP FOUR: *Promotion*

Market Internally: Marketing new services internally is as essential as marketing the service to the community. Health care organizations undertake service programs for seniors for a variety of reasons, and the impetus may come from any of a number of sources, including physicians, nurses, social workers, administrators or trustees.

Many health care organizations are reluctant to branch out beyond traditional health care services. They may be afraid of getting involved in a business they do not know, bringing in senior patients who are difficult and expensive to care for, creating a reputation as a "geriatric institution" with negative connotations, or losing revenues. These fears must be dispelled.

It is important that staff throughout the health care organization understand the rationale for implementing the new program and the potential role that their department may play. Geriatrics is an interdisciplinary program and will effect all components of the hospital in potentially significant ways. Thus, each of the relevant departments must be involved. Seminars, committee meetings, task forces, and individual meetings may be necessary to achieve the commitments of each group.

Marketing to the Community: Publicity, explanation and persuasion to use the new service should begin during the planning stages. This can be done in conjunction with the initial needs assessment: returning to the same sources and making them aware that their suggestions have actually been translated into new programs. Unlike other health care services for which the physicians are the consumers, those that subscribe to services for seniors may be family members, friends, seniors themselves, physicians, the full interdisciplinary complement of health care professionals, clergy, community agencies and anyone else who may interact with older persons. One of the essential aspects of promoting the new service is to convey a positive attitude toward aging. As with the needs assessment, working with the community agencies, such as the Area Agency on Aging and the senior centers, is an efficient way to reach many seniors and to reach healthy, as well as the ill, seniors.

STEP FIVE: *Initiating the Service*

Developing an operating service is a distinct phase that is likely to be done by clinicians and administrators other than those who have been involved in the planning stages of the project. The service initiation requires a specified plan delineating tasks, people responsible, timetables, projected outcomes and evaluation criteria. Critical dimensions pertinent to geriatrics services that may not apply to other services include: structuring the services so that they are integrated with other geriatric services, emphasizing the interdisciplinary approach (and thus involving representatives of all the disciplines), including seniors in the planning and development process, and pricing the services for consumer purchasers.

A word about pricing: many of the services may be different from typical health care services in the way in which overhead is allocated, in the type of regulations that apply, and in the third party reimbursement requirements. Moreover, some services may be paid for primarily by individuals and families directly, and thus must be priced to be compatible with the incomes of the target population. Similar services may be provided by other agencies in the community, some of which may have financial support offsetting costs (such as grants or public allocations) which enables them to charge reduced rates. The health care organization's program must be priced competitively.

STEP SIX: *Evaluate, Revise and Plan*

Returning to the initial concept, marketing "is one of consumers' need orientation backed by integrated marketing aimed at generating consumers satisfaction and long-run consumer welfare as a way to satisfy organizational goals."[20] Consistent with this, an essential step of marketing often neglected is the evaluation and follow-up of the new service. The basic rationale for the detailed marketing approach outlined above is to ensure that the organization has accurately assessed and met the consumers' needs for new services. Meeting consumers' needs should, in turn, enable the organization to meet its own financial or programmatic goals. To evaluate the new service, the health care organization should ask users and potential users of their reactions, their awareness, and their suggestions for modification.

The ideal concept of geriatric services is the continuum of a range of settings. Each service should be developed and evaluated separately. The cost effectiveness of each service also must be assessed. However, one of the distinct features of geriatrics is the integration of services, both in terms of resources used and the effectiveness of care. Thus, each geriatric service should also be assessed for its cost effectiveness relative to its contribution to the spectrum of geriatric care. For example, a home health program may enhance the continuity of care and may financially only break even. However, the availability and ready acceptability of home health may enable a hospital to discharge patients sooner, thus bringing in additional savings as a result of the recent shift to case-based reimbursement.

Long Range Planning: The complexity of initiating geriatric services is one of the very factors which makes it attractive. The array of service opportunities, the need for a continuum of care, and the financial advantages of integrating services offer an opportunity for the health care organization to expand its efforts into additional senior services. The effort put into the initial marketing analysis should thus be expanded into a long-range plan to develop additional related services.

MARKETING FOR THE FUTURE

"Can your company afford to ignore a major uptapped market?"[21] Those over the age of 65 presently comprise 11 percent of the U.S. population and use 33 percent of the dollars spent nationally on health care. The senior population will increase exponentially, growing by at least an additional 50 percent during the coming decade. As the population ages, health care organizations can expect more and more of their patients to be seniors. As is increasingly recognized, the health care needs of older people are highly complex and are different from those of younger adults. The health care organization which begins now to understand and target services oriented toward the special needs of older people and to market them effectively will be well prepared to enter the 21st Century.

FOOTNOTES

1. Philip Kotler, *Marketing for Nonprofit Organizations* (New Jersey: Prentice-Hall, 1975).
2. U.S. Bureau of the Census, Projections of the Population of the United States: 1977 to 2050 *Current Population Reports,* Series P-25 (Washington, D.C.: U.S. Government Printing Office, 1977).
3. U.S. Congress, House, "Percent Growth in Older Population By Age Group," Report on the Subcommittee on Human Services of the Select Committee on Aging, *Future Directions for Aging Policy: A Human Services Model,* 96th Congress, May 1980.

4. *Newsweek,* November 1, 1982.

5. Gerontological Society of America and Western Gerontology Society, *Newer Market—Older People* (Washington, D.C.: GSA, 1983).

6. Janet Schwartz, *Demographic Trends and Hospital Utilization: The Elderly Population,* Office of Public Policy Analysis, Policy Brief Number 41 (Chicago: American Hospital Association, 1982).

7. Schwartz, *Demographic Trends.*

8. Stanley Brody, "Health Care for the Aged," *Hospitals,* May 16, 1980.

9. U.S. Department of Health and Human Services, *Health United States, 1981,* Table 34, DHHS Publication, No. (PHS) 82-1232 (Hyattsville, MD: U.S. Department of Health and Human Services, 1981).

10. Schwartz, *Demographic Trends.*

11. U.S. Dept., *Health, 1981,* Table 44.

12. Health Care Financing Administration, *The Medicare and Medicaid Data Book, 1981* (Washington, D.C.: Department of Health and Human Services, 1982).

13. American Association of Retired Persons, Research and Data Resources Unity, Washington, D.C., 1982.

14. Connie Evashwick, Thomas Rundall, and Betty Goldiamond, *Hospital Services for Older Adults,* to be published in *The Gerontologist,* 1984.

15. Bernice Neugarten, *Older Americans: A Profile of Social Health Characteristics,* in The Hospital Research and Educational Trust, *The Hospital's Role in Caring for the Elderly: Leadership Issues* (Chicago: The Trust, 1982).

16. National Center for Health Statistics, *National Health Interview Survey,* Department of Health and Human Services, Public Health Service, Washington, D.C.

17. U.S. Bureau of the Census, *Current Population Reports,* Series P-60, No. 126, Table 7 (Washington, D.C.: Government Printing Office, 1979).

18. U.S. Bureau, *Current Reports.*

19. Jeffrey Pope, *Practical Marketing Research* (New York: AMACOM 1981).

20. American College of Hospital Administrators, *Marketing Seminar Workbook,* 1981.

21. Gerontology Society of America and the Western Gerontology Society (Washington, D.C.: GSA, 1983).

Increasing Competition Will Expand the Healthcare Marketer's Role

Joseph B. McCarthy, B.S., M.B.A., M.S.
Lily L. Hurlimann, B.A., M.B.A.

Rapid healthcare cost inflation in the United States in recent years has alarmed both government and private payors. One consequence is a movement toward freer competition, as exemplified by the California healthcare marketplace since 1982. To the extent that the competitive model applies to a given situation, the nature of applied healthcare marketing and the role of the healthcare marketer will be significantly affected.

This article draws upon the experience of the authors in observing the direct consequences of certain health legislation which was passed in California in 1982. These legislative changes pushed both the Medicaid program (called Medi-Cal in California) and the private health insurance industry toward the competitive model. While the discussion and examples which follow relate largely to our experience in the general acute hospital setting, it is felt that parallel developments can be anticipated for the pre-acute and post-acute segments of the health delivery system.

Joseph B. McCarthy is Director of Planning for Seton Medical Center in Daly City, California. Prior to his position at Seton, Mr. McCarthy was Director of Planning and Marketing at Saint Francis Memorial Hospital in San Francisco. Earlier in his career he held positions in the management consulting field. Mr. McCarthy holds a B.S. degree in Marketing from the University of Illinois, an M.B.A. in Marketing from Northwestern University, and an M.S. in Health Planning from the University of California, Los Angeles.

Lily L. Hurlimann is the Assistant Director of Planning for Seton Medical Center in Daly City, California. Prior to this position, she was Reimbursement Specialist with Brigham and Women's Hospital, Boston, Massachusetts. Earlier, she served with the Massachusetts Rate Setting Commission as Director of Development, Prospective Reimbursement System. Ms. Hurlimann holds an M.B.A. in Health Care Administration from Boston University, and an B.A. from Tufts University.

ENVIRONMENTAL FORCES

In recent years, healthcare cost inflation in the U.S. has greatly outstripped overall inflation, as evidenced by the following trends:

— Total healthcare expenditures in the U.S. increased from 7.6 percent of the gross national product in 1970, to 10.5 percent in 1982. By 1982, healthcare expenditures in the U.S. totalled $324 billion or $1,365 per capita.
— Federal Medicare outlays, which totalled $9.5 billion in 1973, are projected to total $57.3 billion in 1983, an increase of over 500 percent during the decade.
— The U.S. Chamber of Commerce estimates that about 12.5 percent of a typical company's payroll was required to cover health costs in 1982, compared to only 7.0 percent in 1970; during this period business health expenditures increased 700 percent, almost three and one-half times the increase in GNP.

This rapid inflation in the health care sector of the U.S. economy in recent years has resulted in growing pressures for containment of health expenditures. Alarmed by these increasing health costs, the major financiers of healthcare—government, employers, and private insurance companies—have begun to implement serious countermeasures. For example, the federal government is implementing a prospective payment system for Medicare which is based upon a regionally adjusted schedule for prices for a list of 468 diagnostic-related groups (i.e. DRGs). Meanwhile, individual states have acted to limit public and private health expenditures using a variety of approaches ranging from increased regulation on one hand to increased competition on the other hand. At the same time, employers are attempting to contain health-related expenditures by shifting an increasing proportion of costs to employees (e.g., higher premium contributions; higher co-payment and deductibles).

STATE-LEVEL RESPONSES

At the state level, a variety of legislation has been initiated recently to contain healthcare costs. In certain cases, there have been movements toward imposing order in the healthcare marketplace through increased regulatory controls. For example, West Virginia,

Wisconsin and Maine recently enacted legislation establishing rate setting programs. Furthermore, in 1982 Massachusetts and New York implemented systems controlling hospital charges for all third-party payors. This type of extensive regulation tends to move the healthcare industry toward the role of a public utility.

Other state-level responses have been directed toward controlling health costs through pressures associated with freer competition within the healthcare marketplace. For example, in 1982 the California legislature passed two companion bills, AB 799 and AB 3480, which allow the state Medicaid program (i.e. Medi-Cal) as well as private insurers to negotiate specific payment levels with individual hospitals and physicians. As one result, the Medi-Cal program has initiated a competitive bidding process wherein many acute hospitals throughout the state lost virtually all of their Medi-Cal business to hospitals which made successful bids. Meanwhile, the recent legislation has provided impetus to the private health insurance industry to respond with a variety of "preferred provider organization" (PPO) initiatives. Under the PPO approach, insurance carriers negotiate contracts with select panels of hospitals and physicians, and provide strong incentives to PPO-plan subscribers/beneficiaries to choose panel providers. As a case in point, Blue Cross in California recently inaugurated a PPO, called the Prudent Buyer Plan, which is being marketed as a lower-cost addition to Blue Cross's traditional indemnity coverage.

It is too early to judge whether regulation or competition will be more successful in containing health costs in a manner acceptable to the American public. However, the competitive system in California is worth examining because it has dramatic implications for the future of healthcare marketing. If the competitive system proves effective, it could be replicated, in whole or in part, nationwide.

REQUIREMENTS FOR PRICE COMPETITION

In the past, competition among health service providers has largely involved factors other than price. This is due to the fact that third-party payors have tended to insulate individual users of health services from the direct expenses associated with their utilization patterns. For example, typical co-payment and deductible provisions of employer-sponsored indemnity health insurance plans require the users to pay only a small fraction of the total expenditures which they incur. In the absence of intense price competition in the healthcare marketplace, other forms of competition have developed. Providers have competed, at times intensely, in terms of factors such as reputation for quality, ease of access, and attractiveness of facilities.

In direct contrast to historical patterns, the California healthcare marketplace is moving rapidly toward price competition. Price sensitivity for reimbursable health services can only occur if the groups paying the price—government and private insurers—have some control over the decision on how to spend the health dollars. There are three characteristics of the California health environment which allow the third-parties to influence prices. The first two exist as a result of the 1982 California legislation (AB 799 and AB 3480), while the third characteristic is simply the result of the normal competitive marketplace at work.

1. The payors have the authority and incentive to influence the subscribers'/beneficiaries' choice of health provider. This means the payor allows the subscriber only limited choice of hospitals and physicians, or provides strong financial incentives (e.g., by reducing or eliminating premium contributions, deductibles and/or co-payment) to use selected cost-effective providers. By limiting access, payors can direct larger numbers of patients to lower-cost providers. Historically, limitations on freedom-of-choice have been confined largely to health maintenance organizations (HMOs). Under typical circumstances, government payors (i.e. Medicaid and Medicare) in the past were not permitted to limit beneficiaries' freedom to select providers. Meanwhile, commercial insurers had little economic incentive to restrict choice as long as employers continued to pay the high priced health premiums. However, in California Medi-Cal was granted a federal waiver in 1982 exempting the State from the usual Medicaid freedom-of-choice provisions. At the same time, commercial insurers in California, fearing hospitals and physicians would increase charges to offset Medi-Cal revenue loss because of competitive bidding, found they had a strong economic incentive to develop policies restricting patient access to only the lower-charge providers. Moreover, the 1982 competitive health legislation in California greatly facilitated such initiatives by commercial insurers.

2. The payors have the authority to negotiate prices with the hospitals and physicians. In most states the private insurers are simply "price takers." In these circumstances, private insurers do not negotiate with specific hospitals; rather, they accept prices set by hospitals or by a regulatory agency. Furthermore, in most states Medicaid reimbursement is based upon complicated cost formulas supported by extensive and explicit regulations. In California, however, all commercial insurers and Medi-Cal now have the right to negotiate contracts with the providers. Payment levels, payment mechanisms and virtually any other terms of the contract are open to negotiation.

3. There is excess hospital capacity with few monopoly situations in most geographic areas. California hospitals, on average, have been operating well below optimum occupancy levels. In addition, few hospitals have a monopoly position in their market. The payors can exercise significant leverage over individual hospitals by simply terminating negotiations and contracting with a competitor. Few hospitals can afford to lose a substantial proportion of their business to a competitor.

These three factors combined allow the payors to deliver increased numbers of patients to contract hospitals in exchange for sizable discounts. Hospitals that are unwilling to negotiate may lose access to a large portion of the patient population, while hospitals who negotiate successfully could significantly increase their share of the market.

SUCCESSFUL CONTRACTING

The hospital with a high probability of long-term survival in an intensively competitive environment, characterized by price-sensitive contracting, might be described as one that:

— Identifies, analyzes, and manages its various major "product lines."
— Aggressively markets the hospital (and its medical staff) to the numerous marketing entities and intermediaries who are emerging as "buyers" of health care.
— Effectively monitors and controls costs, utilization, and quality of services.
— Develops appropriate linkages to insure that the hospital is part of a comprehensive network of health services.

Major steps that are suggested to improve a hospital's marketing effectiveness in a contracting environment are described below.

1. Develop a marketing information base. Adequate information is required to accurately assess an organization's current market position, and to identify market oppotunities. For example, the information base should include a profile of major HMOs, PPOs, and various insurance carriers serving residents of the area. In addition, other providers in the service area should be assessed in terms of competitive strengths and vulnerabilities, and possible marketing affiliations should be evaluated. Moreover, working definitions for major "product lines" (i.e., comprehensive services, provided to distinct categories of patients, such as: oncology services; cardiology services; perinatal services; etc.) should be established and, in each case, revenues, costs and net profitability should be analyzed.

2. Establish a contracting strategy. A specific marketing strategy related to contracting would address issues such as the relative marketing emphasis to be placed upon various types of contracting entities and intermediaries, (e.g., insurance carriers, PPOs, HMOs) including estimates of volume targets. In addition, the strategy should include a systematic approach to screening carriers and to reviewing the legal and operational implications of proposed contracts. Moreover, the strategy should define an approach to various reimbursement schemes such as: standard per diems; fixed amount per discharge; percent discount off charges; etc. Furthermore, a workable and internally consistent pricing policy, including profitability targets and volume discounts, should be established. Finally, specific strategy for conducting detailed negotiations should be developed.

3. Establish and maintain relationships with contracting entities. Initially, contracting in California (i.e., with Medi-Cal, and Blue Cross) followed an open process in which all hospitals had an equal opportunity to participate in bidding. More recent experience suggests that the marketplace is becoming more secretive, with various contracting entities and providers selectively approaching each other. Under these circumstances, a strong element of personal salesmanship is needed in order to maximize favorable bidding opportunities, to develop persuasive bid packages, and to maintain ongoing relationships with contracting entities.

4. Strengthen medical staff relationships. A hospital's success in the contracting environment will be critically dependent upon a productive and mutually supportive relationship with its medical staff. Typically, a contracting entity would negotiate a hospital contract along with separate contracts with participating medical staff members. However, the ability of a hospital to deliver cost-effective quality care at a profitable level is largely dependent upon physician decision-making with respect to admissions, ordering of diagnostic and treatment services, discharges, etc. At the same time, physicians can benefit in the competitive environment by associating with an attractive and efficient hospital which markets itself and its medical staff aggressively.

5. *Develop linkages with compatible providers.* To remain competitive in the health insurance marketplace, contracting entities such as HMOs and PPOs are generally interested in forming regional networks of providers which cover broad geographic areas. Under these circumstances, the individual hospital could benefit by linking formally or informally with compatible, non-competing hospitals in the area. Moreover, to improve cost-effectiveness, it may be useful for a hospital to establish formal linkages with nursing homes, home care agencies, etc., to facilitate prompt discharge from the more expensive acute care setting.

6. *Establish evaluation and control mechanisms.* Hospitals entering the contracting environment are advised to establish various feedback mechanisms to maximize learning and to insure that appropriate corrections are made early. For example, customer satisfaction with services rendered, adherence to billing procedures, etc., should be continually evaluated. In addition, profitability by contract entity and product line should be monitored.

ORGANIZATIONAL IMPLICATIONS

If hospitals are to accomplish the numerous tasks associated with successful contracting, they must make certain organizational adaptations to the price-competitive environment. In responsive institutions, the marketing function will encompass broader responsibilities and will become more systematized.

Recent History of Healthcare Marketing

Only in recent years has institutional healthcare marketing emerged as a recognized field. In the late 1970's, only a relatively few progressive hospitals created formal marketing positions. The trend appears to have accelerated in the 1980's.

As might be expected, given the recent emergence of the position, the role of the institutional healthcare marketer is often limited in terms of range of activities and scope of responsibilities. This assessment is supported by a recent survey by Witt & Associates of about 800 non-government hospitals (from a total sample of about 5,000). In this study, those executives primarily responsible for marketing were queried regarding functional responsibilities and activities. The study results suggest that hospital executives primarily responsible for the marketing within individual institutions tend to have limited marketing background and experience. Moreover, these executives have marginal control over many responsibilities typically associated with marketing. For example, only ten percent of respondents control advertising; only nine percent were responsible for new service/product development; only seven percent managed physician relations activities; and only three percent of the marketing executives controlled pricing decisions.

It appears that the typical hospital marketing executive does not have the authority and the decision-making responsibility commonly found among marketing executives in the private sector. This limitation is compounded by the sheer diversity and complexity of the health services marketplace. Thus, there appear to be significant opportunities for the enhancement of the role of healthcare marketers.

Shift in Emphasis Under Price Competition

Historically, there has been a tendency for healthcare marketing to operate under the assumption that individual patients generally have broad freedom of choice regarding selection of a personal physician and/or hospital. Under a price-competitive environment, we can expect the role of healthcare marketing to shift toward a pattern more typical of industrial firms within the private sector. For example, the role of intermediaries, or marketing "channels," will become more important. As a growing proportion of the population comes under HMO and PPO coverage, individuals' freedom of choice regarding selection of physicians and hospitals will be significantly restricted. Meanwhile, health providers will increasingly establish contractual relationships with various third-party payors in order to capture potentially large patient populations on a long-term basis at pre-negotiated rates.

Examples of New Functional Responsibilities for Marketing

The emergence of price competition will provide an opportunity for healthcare marketers to assume additional functional responsibilities, such as those identified below:

1. *Program management.* It is not uncommon for consumer goods firms to have brand managers responsible for the overall marketing performance of specific product lines. It is expected that increasing competition will spur health organizations to move toward program management systems. As DRG-type data systems continue to develop (in response to recent Medicare reimbursement changes), it is becoming possible to regularly monitor and control the profit and loss associated with program areas such as oncology, cardiology, etc. A strong case can be made that program managers should report to the primary marketing executive.

2. *Direct sales.* Historically, hospitals have tended to take a somewhat passive attitude toward customers. Under competition, it is clear that direct sales will become increasingly important to health organizations, as they seek to actively increase sales volume and market share. As an example, Seton Medical Center in Daly City, California has recently organized a three-person sales force responsible for facilitating the growth of programs such as: alcoholism treatment; executive fitness; and home health.

3. *Physician relations.* Historically, hospitals have viewed their medical staffs as the primary market, in recognition of physicians' ability to direct patients to hospitals. The contracting environment will tend to change this perspective somewhat. In a sense, a hospital and its medical staff members could be viewed as joint-venturers who collaborate in establishing various relationships with contracting entities. There is an opportunity for the marketer to assume an active role in developing such joint-venture relationships with the medical staff.

4. *Contract development.* If recent California experience is an indication, the marketing function within health organizations appears to be evolving toward an emphasis upon the development and maintenance of long-term relationships with major contracting entities (with HMOs, PPOs, employers, other providers, etc.). In a price-competitive marketplace, much of a hospital's indemnity insurance business is "up for grabs." In these circumstances, it can be expected that many individuals currently insured by indemnity carriers will convert from standard indemnity coverage to restricted PPO and HMO options. Unless the hospital has hedged its bet by capturing a representative proportion of the growing PPO and HMO business, its market share will decline. On the other hand, to the extent the hospital does a better-than-average job in securing PPO and HMO contracts, its market share will increase. Marketing effort ex-

panded in this area can be very highly profitable in terms of dollar results. As a case in point, it is not uncommon for individual insurance carriers to account for upwards of a million dollars or more of annual gross revenues of a larger acute hospital.

Under these circumstances, a formal approach to prospect development, proposal writing and presentation, pricing strategy, account servicing, etc., will be required. Thus, there are expanding opportunities in the health care marketplace for individuals who acquire and maintain contract business. In larger hospitals, the magnitude of this contract development task could easily require the creation of a full-time position. For example, two hospitals in the San Francisco Bay Area have recently created specific positions designed to generate and service major contract business. Saint Francis Memorial Hospital in San Francisco has full-time Contract Manager. Similarly, Seton Medical Center, in suburban Daly City, has created the full-time position of Director of Contract Development.

SUMMARY AND CONCLUSIONS

In recent years, healthcare cost inflation in the U.S. has greatly outstripped overall inflation. Alarmed by these rapidly increasing health costs, the major financiers of healthcare have begun to implement serious countermeasures. For example, the federal government is implementing a prospective payment system based upon the DRG approach. Meanwhile, individual states have acted to limit public and private health expenditures using a variety of approaches ranging from increased regulation on one hand to increased competition on the other hand. At the same time, employers are attempting to contain health-related expenditures by shifting an increasing proportion of costs to employees.

The movement toward freer competition is exemplified recently by the California healthcare marketplace. In 1982, California passed legislation which allowed the State Medicaid program (called Medi-Cal) as well as private insurers to negotiate specific payment levels with individual hospitals and physicians. As a result, the Medi-Cal program implemented a competitive bidding process with providers, while the private insurance companies responded with a variety of preferred provider organization (PPO) initiatives. With these developments, the California marketplace possesses the three key elements for price competition: first, the payors have the authority and incentive to influence the subscribers'/beneficiaries' choice of health provider; second, the payors have the authority to negotiate prices with the hospitals and physicians; third, there is excess hospital capacity with few monopoly situations in most geographic areas. The competitive system in California is worth examining because it has dramatic implications for the future of healthcare marketing. Moreover, if the competitive system proves effective, it could be replicated throughout the nation.

To survive over the long-term in an intensely price-competitive environment, a hospital must develop an effective marketing program. Major steps toward that end should include:

— Developing a marketing information base in order to accurately assess the organizations' current market position and to identify market opportunities.
— Establishing a systematic contracting strategy which addresses target markets, carrier evaluation, alternative reimbursement schemes, pricing policy, and negotiating approach.
— Establishing and maintaining ongoing relationships with various contracting entities.
— Strengthening medical staff relationships in order to develop joint-venture partnership approaches to various contracting opportunities.
— Developing and maintaining network linkages with noncompeting and complimentary providers.
— Establishing evaluation and control mechanisms to maximize learning and to allow appropriate corrections to be made early.

If hospitals are to accomplish the numerous tasks associated with successful contracting, they must make certain organizational adaptations to the price-competitive environment. In responsive institutions, the marketing function with encompass broader responsibilities and will be more systemetized. For example, the chief marketing executive might assume additional functional responsibilities such as: marketing management of programs or "product lines"; direct sales; physician relations; and contract development.

In conclusion, the shift toward competition in the healthcare marketplace is subject to great uncertainties and regional variations. To the extent the competitive model proves effective, it will likely be replicated. This development would profoundly change the nature of healthcare marketing. At the same time, the move toward competition poses great opportunities for enhancing the healthcare marketer's role.

REFERENCES

"A History of Achievement, A Future With Promise: The Health Maintenance Industry Ten-Year Report, 1973-83," National Industry Council for HMO Development, Washington, D.C., 1983.

"Preferred Provider Organization Contracting Manual: Issues and Strategies," Hospital Council of Northern California, San Bruno, May 1983.

Richards, Glenn, "Headline of the '80s: This Is Supposed To Be the Decade of Competition. Will It Be?" *Hospitals,* July 16, 1983, pp. 110-116.

Witt, John A., and Nelson L. McRoberts, "Marketing Competition: Lack of Expertise, Funding Shackles Marketing Moves," *Modern Healthcare,* April 1983, pp. 75-78.

The Medical Marketing Audit:
A Technique for Today's Competitive
Extended Care Environment

Albert V. Aguiar

One seasoned Health Care observer recently noted that you could place all extended care facilities in one of two categories when it came to marketing:

1. Those who have no formalized Marketing Program and feel uncertain about their position, and
2. Those who are doing some type of Marketing and feel uncertain about their position.

Although there is undoubtedly a certain amount of exaggeration in the above statements, there is also more than a little truth involved. Most extended care facilities feel uncertain about Marketing whether they're involved in it or not. Sometimes this uncertainty postpones or prevents the start of even a modest marketing program. Other times uncertainty leads to a perpetration of inappropriate and/or unproductive marketing programs.

Just as we regularly assess and review the medical and operational aspects of our practices, we need to make a solid *marketing* assessment of what we're doing. We cannot afford to guess whether what we're doing is right. In these changing, competitive times we need to *know*. Other than management judgment and intuition, is there some way to objectively make this type of assessment? The answer is a definite "yes" and the technique that is best used for this purpose is called a *marketing audit*.

Albert V. Aguiar is Director, Graduate Program in Marketing, Golden Gate University; President, Al Aguiar & Associates.

45

WHAT IS A MARKETING AUDIT?

A *Marketing Audit* is an independent, knowledgeable assessment of *all* the elements of the business from a *marketing* point of view. It includes a tough assessment of the services being offered *as viewed by the patient,* a review of the internal procedures in place that contribute or detract from practice development, a marketing "I.Q." review of the staff, plus a complete examination of whatever external marketing programs may be in place.

Although the concept of a marketing audit is fairly new in the medical field, the idea has been around for at least 10 years in other fields. Fundamentally, the marketing audit owes its beginning to the accounting profession, where the concept of a financial audit has long had complete industry acceptance. The idea behind regular financial auditing is quite simple: even though you *may* have honest, qualified people handling your finances, it's important to have an independent review of the process occasionally to confirm the correctness of the regular procedures, point out possible irregularities and identify areas for possible improvement.

In most larger organizations top managers are not qualified and/or don't have the time to do their own financial audits. The outside independent financial audit, therefore, becomes a necessity.

Many of the same things that make a financial audit a necessity also make marketing audits highly desireable for most health services organizations. Most health service administrators/proprietors are *not* professionaly schooled as marketing specialists. In addition to the usual time limitations, most individuals managing health care facilities find it difficult to be completely objective when it comes to evaluating the level of competence that exists in an inexact area such as marketing.

WHAT SHOULD BE INCLUDED IN THE AUDIT?

Although the specific list of items is virtually endless, there are a few major "blocks" of non-medical factors that should be covered in every marketing audit:

Patient Population Analysis. Before you can reasonably assess how well an organization is doing in its marketing, you must first know some very specific information about the patients you are servicing. The analysis should examine a variety of factors including, but not limited to: age of patients, sex, income and/or source of funds, ethnic background, permanent residence before becoming a patient, social and/or occupational background, how they learned about your services, etc. This information will be compared to a typical patient profile for your type of service in your community.

Preliminary Patient Impressions. How does your facility look from a physical standpoint, both inside and out? What are the impressions based upon neighborhood, surrounding buildings, etc.? How does lighting, color, furnishings, etc. affect the first impression?

Preliminary Impression of Personnel. How do your people look? How do they dress? What is their in-person presence? Do they *appear* to be competent and businesslike? How supportive of the practice do they appear to be?

Process and Procedures. How much "red tape" is involved in servicing your patients? Are services, pricing, etc. easy for the *patient* to understand? Have you eliminated as much technical and medical jargon from the paperwork that the patient or his family must read and understand? Is the administrative process planned as much as possible for the convenience of the *patient* and his family, as opposed to your own convenience?

Staff Marketing I.Q. A successful marketing program *has* to begin with the people in the organization. How aware are they of marketing? Do they understand the difference between marketing and selling? Do they understand the positive benefits that marketing can bring to the practice? Do they realize that there are some positive benefits that marketing can bring in terms of quality patient care? Does everyone understand the marketing goals of the organization and their own role in accomplishing these goals?

Referral Program. Perhaps the best and most productive method for getting new patients is through a well developed referral program. What is the source of your new patient referrals? Are referrals increasing or decreasing? Do you have an active program in place to encourage referrals from your existing patients and their families? What techniques do you use to find new sources of medical referrals? What specific programs do you have in place of acknowledging and encouraging the individuals who now refer to you?

Community Outreach. It is important that you be well known in the community. What is being done to increase the ongoing visibility of the organization in the community? How active or involved are the key members of the organization in community affairs? What program or programs have been developed to present information on extended care to service groups or other organizations in the community? How well known is your organization in educational circles in your community? How does the community outreach program that your organization has in place compare with that of competitors in the same general area?

Other Non-personal External Marketing Efforts. Under this category we include everything else that is being done outside of your facility except those things that are being done on an individual or face-to-face basis. Certainly we would include all types of traditional advertising here, but we would also include such things as phone directory listings, press releases, newsletters, external publication, etc.

WHO SHOULD DO THE MARKETING AUDIT?

If the marketing audit is to truly be an *audit* and not a self-examination, someone *outside* of your day to day practice should conduct it. It is not absolutely necessary that the individual be well versed in your particular type of extended care practice. They must, however, understand management and have a strong bias for quality care *from the patient's viewpoint.* Ideally, they should know a *little* about medical care and a *lot* about marketing.

Although the above paragraph would seem to strongly suggest bringing in a marketing consultant, it's certainly not mandatory to do so. What *is* mandatory is that the administrator, president, or other individual with direct proprietory interest *not* conduct the audit. In a smaller facility it is possible that a graduate marketing student, with proper guidance, might be able to conduct a simple audit. You should try to get the best quality audit you can but you should realize, however, that even a preliminary marketing audit which does not examine every aspect of the practice is much better than no audit at all. The important objective here is to obtain whatever information you can and to obtain it from an impartial source.

HOW DO YOU GET STARTED?

The first step, of course, is to make the decision that you want the audit. The marketing audit is, in a sense, a form of independent introspective marketing research. Like any other type of marketing research it should only be undertaken if you are willing to seriously consider the results and initiate action based upon those results. This doesn't mean you shouldn't ask questions or challenge some of the findings, if appropriate. What it *does* mean is that if you're not willing to consider changes in your overall marketing effort there's no reason to spend time, effort, or money doing a marketing audit.

Once you've definitely decided to have a marketing audit done you can then get on with the business of finding someone to do it. You may already know someone with the general qualifications outlined earlier. If not, ask some of your peers with whom you're not directly competing. Some medical practice management companies offer the service; most do not. If you have to explain what you mean by a medical marketing audit, you're probably talking to the wrong company. Don't be discouraged if you don't find the right individual immediately . . . it's worth the effort.

When you find someone who seems to understand what you want and seems competent to perform the audit, ask a lot more questions. What is it exactly that the auditor will deliver to you? How long will the audit take? Who will be involved with it within your organization? How much of their time will be involved? Finally, how much will it cost and on what basis is the cost determined? Be sure you understand what is being provided and that the auditor knows in as much detail as possible what it is that *you* expect.

IN CONCLUSION

Marketing audits in the medical field *are* rather new and, therefore, a little difficult for most administrators and proprietors to objectively assess in terms of probable effectiveness before actually undertaking them. As with all new techniques there is not a large body of data confirming how they have been used and the results that have been achieved.

As with many marketing techniques the effectiveness of marketing audits tends to vary depending upon the skill of the marketer *and* the degree of commitment from the organization involved. Decision making is not a fool-proof science. The quality of decision making can, however, be improved by the quality and objectivity of information that is available. In this respect, there is no doubt that a good marketing audit can improve the quality of marketing decision making. The Medical Marketing Audit *is* a technique whose time has come.

Positioning the Long-Term and Senior Care Service in the Minds of the Medical Provider and Consumer

William J. Winston

INTRODUCTION TO MARKET POSITIONING

One of the most important aspects of marketing a health and human service is the use of market positioning. Positioning is an attempt to distinguish the human service or organization from its competitors along real dimensions in order to be the preferred service to select segments of the marketplace. Positioning aims to educate the medical provider or consumer about the real differences between alternative human services. This differentiation assists providers and consumers in matching themselves to the service that can be of most value. The tool of positioning is 1) image-making; 2) perception-oriented; and 3) personality-directed.

Positioning is not necessarily a new tool in marketing. Historically, the concept of positioning was mainly concerned with what marketers did to the service or product being marketed. Today, it mainly means what the marketer does for the service or product in the provider's or customer's mind. The original aspect of positioning was derived from 'product positioning' which utilized the product's physical appearance, size, form and price compared to its competitors. Today, it is important to market the organization's image, but it is vital to create a position in the provider's or customer's mind. The following questions need to be answered in order to lay the groundwork for positioning strategies:

William J. Winston is Dean and Assistant Professor of Management, School of Health Services Management, Golden Gate University San Francisco, CA; Managing Associate, Professional Services Marketing Group, a health marketing consulting firm, San Francisco, CA.

1. HOW IS MY SERVICE CURRENTLY PERCEIVED BY THE MARKETPLACE?
2. WHAT DO I WANT MY PROVIDERS/CLIENTS TO THINK OF MY SERVICES?
3. WHAT ARE THE WEAKNESSES AND STRENGTHS OF MY SERVICES?
4. HAVE I EMPHASIZED THE SERVICE'S STRENGTHS AND CAN I IMPROVE THE WEAKNESSES?
5. WHAT ARE THE STRENGTHS AND WEAKNESSES OF MY COMPETITORS?
6. WHAT IS THE 'POSITIONING GAP' THAT IS APPARENT IN MY COMPETITORS' SERVICES AND HOW CAN I FILL THE GAP WITH MY SERVICES?
7. HOW CAN I INFLUENCE THE PROSPECTIVE OR EXISTING PROVIDER/CLIENT TO PERCEIVE MY SERVICES RELATED TO MY POSITION?

All of these questions lay the framework for the development of a **POSITIONING STRATEGY.** The positioning strategy describes what your service stands for; how you would like providers/clients to evaluate your services; and how you will communicate the **POSITIONING PERCEPTION** of the services to your providers and clients. Communicating the positioning statement to your marketplace is important yet difficult since our society is over communicated to within a very crowded marketplace. Today's health care marketplace is no longer responsive to the strategies that worked in the past. There are just too many products, services, organizations, and marketing messages. In our overcommunicated society, there is a strong need to be selective and concentrate on specific target groups and communicate to these groups using narrowly defined strategies. One of these key marketing strategies is 'positioning' your service in the minds of the medical provider or the health consumer.

ENVIRONMENTAL CHANGES FOR TARGETING THE SENIOR CARE MARKETPLACE

Long-term and senior care citizens will double in size during the next twenty years. Growing numbers of senior citizens will demand an expanding array of elderly and geriatric services. Long-term care is already changing to become not just related to facility-type services in nursing homes. It has become a 'continuum of care' which includes skilled nursing facilities, hospices, intermediate care centers, mental health centers, home health care programs, congregate living centers, respite care, recreational programs, and day care. The increasing demand for services and the creation of these innovative new services cause new challenges for long-term and senior care administrators. Highly trained and motivated health care professionals will be needed to meet this challenge since long term care may well be the major health and social issue of the next four decades. The resource needs of long-term and senior care will be competing fiercely with those of defense, education, energy, and welfare. Long-term and senior care is a unique and pervasive part of our society. Unfortunately, recent fiscal and demographic realities have only recently forced society to start to define clear goals for it. These major concerns will require the development of improved communication between the senior care programs and their medical providers or consumers. Along with other management tools of financial analysis, human resource management, strategic planning, policy analysis, and economic analysis, marketing will be playing a major role in enhancing and creating an improved communication network.

The dimensions of long-term and senior care services are rooted within the demographic changes of our society. For example, one in every five Americans will be 65 years of age or older by the year 2030 as the baby boom generation ages and life expectancy grows. The U.S. Census Dept. predicts that there will be over 64 million people age 65 or older by the year 2030 out of a total population of 304 million. Today, there are 27 million Americans over age 65. The enormous demographic shift crossed a watershed in July, 1983 when for the first time in American history, people over 65 outnumbered teenagers.

The following pieces of information reinforce how dramatic these changes really are:

—The 65 and over segment of the population grew twice as fast as the rest of the population in the last 20 years;
—The 85-and-over group is growing rapidly, up 165 percent in 22 years;
—The death rate of the elderly population, especially of women, fell considerably over the last 40 years;

— Despite gains in the median income of the elderly in the past two decades, about one in every seven Americans over the age of 65 lives in poverty;
— Elderly women are almost twice as likely as elderly men to be poor. Half the elderly widowed black women live in poverty;
— Social Security benefits reach 91% of the elderly population, with the benefits accounting for half the total cash income of half those people;
— Three out of four elderly people die of heart disease, cancer or stroke. Heart disease remains the major cause of death;
— Longevity is no longer the chief cause of the current growth of the older population. The prime reason is the steady increase in the number of births up to the age of 40;
— Births, after dropping through 1940, began to rise during the post-World War II baby boom; slowed down during the late 1960s and early 1970s; and now has re-accelerated; and
— Life expectancy at the turn of the century was 49 years; by 1954 it had risen to 70 years of age; by 1974 it had risen to 74 years; and it is expected that by 2050 women can expect to live to 84 years, and men to 82 years.

Since long-term and senior care services are very much a function of advancing age, demographic reality just outlined presents the United States and the long-term care industry with extraordinary tasks in terms of money, providing services, and marketing their services during the next forty years. Marketing will be important for communicating with these population groups; medical providers who need to provide advice and referrals to long-term and senior care services; and to government officials and health planners who need to address health policy decisions regarding this important change in our society.

There has already been a tremendous increase in the number and types of services available for the elderly. The increase in alternative modes of delivery and services supports the need for improved communication about the uniqueness of our services. The long-term and senior care marketplace is gradually becoming overcrowded and overcommunicated. The following list provides an indication of the complexity in differentiating our specific services within an overcrowded marketplace. These types of services already exist. The list will probably triple during the next twenty years. Services that senior citizens can choose from include:

IN-HOME SERVICES: homemaker/home health care/nutrition programs/monitoring services

COMMUNITY SERVICES: legal services/protective services/senior centers/nutritional programs/Dental/Mental Health/Adult Day Care/Respite Care/Hospice Care/Recreational

and

INSTITUTIONAL SERVICES: Respite Care/hospice care/retirement villages/domiciliary care/foster home/personal care home/congregate homes/skilled nursing care/intermediate care/mental hospitals/acute care hospitals, etc.

GENERAL IMPACT ON MARKETING

The proliferation of new services and increasing demand for these services require the need for long-term and senior care administrators to 'POSITION' their services in the minds of the medical providers and consumers it serves. Marketers within the long-term and senior care industry, as well as marketers in all consumer markets, will be making a stronger effort to reach the older population groups. For example, older models will grace advertising of diverse products—not just laxatives, denture creams and arthritis painkillers. Packages will feature bigger print and more product information. And foods will continue to stress nutrition. The appearance and content of food will also change for the older population. Campbell Soup Co., for example, has already begun to specifically target its low-sodium and single-serving products to senior citizens. Traditionally, the 18-35 age group has held the most purchasing power. But with many senior citizens returning to the work force, they will have more disposable income.

The maturing of the American population has increased the dollar value of the consumer marketplace for the mature population to over $400 billion a year. This marketplace is quite different than previous target groups. Educational levels of the senior citizen group will be considerably higher than in the past and marketers of consumer products will need to change their direction. Smart selling will have to replace hard selling that tends to attract younger population groups. Products/services will need to be marketed using more detailed information about the products or services. The senior citizen group will, for example, not as readily accept new services or products as the younger groups. In other words, it will be very difficult to con the maturity market. This group will be less gullible. Proven products/services and word of mouth referrals will be selected. Peer group pressure to try something just because it is new or innovative will not be an effective strategy.

The maturity market comprises at least 44 million individuals and one-third of all households. This group is quality-oriented. Older persons are more likely to demand quality and reasonably long life for products or services and are much less likely to care about purchasing the latest model or style of product/service. Gimmicks will not be successful with these groups. Advertising, for example, will have to become more truthful. However, there is a tremendous hangover from the youth orientation in our society. Marketers still concentrate on the premise that youth suggests excitement and glamor while older segments of the population are dowdy and uninspiring. This premise represents the major transition that will occur in marketing to the maturing population. Gradually, it will make more economic sense because this older group holds more promise for a wide range of consumer products/services than do the young.

Another key application is the maturing of America's impact on the world of business. Among the concerns are the relationship between worker productivity and age; retraining of the displaced older worker; orienting technology for the older worker; developing alternatives to full-time retirement and enhanced financial planning; evaluating whether wellness programs are cost-effective for older workers within the workplace; and managerial sensitivity training when dealing with the mature worker's needs. A key use of marketing will be for educating and soliciting participation by mature workers in health promotion and wellness programs within businesses or community. Employers are becoming increasingly concerned with the health problems of men and women over the age of 65. It is estimated that over sixty percent of retired workers, for example, remain eligible for some type of employer related group health insurance coverage. Pre-retirement wellness programs may be a methodology to reduce absenteeism, improve productivity, and thus, enhance cost-containment within businesses. It seems reasonable to assume that in time there will be an expanded use of mature workers. Employment opportunities probably will develop new forms different from the traditional eight-hour day. Flexible scheduling and home projects may be stimulated and become part of these wellness programs.

Another example of impacts on marketing can be demonstrated by the recent interest of major hotel chains in attracting the mature population. For example, Ramada Inns have discovered that senior citizens comprise a huge and largely untapped market of sophisticated people with money to spend and time to spend it. Ramada Inns is giving seniors a discount of around 15% for room rates. The company reasons that seniors can comprise a significant volume of business and that businesses need to erase the myth among employees that seniors cannot enjoy themselves. Ramada has researched that a person 55 years of age or older spends an average of 7.3 nights away from home per trip and consumes about one out of every ten lunches and dinners served at most restaurants. In addition, they found that about 80% of the money in savings and loan associations is held by a person 55 years of age or older. The company projects that this group wants to spend these sums on themselves. Some of the marketing techniques the hotel chain has used include the scenario that seniors appreciate efficient service, but dislike the high-speed check-in, check-out tactics preferred by hurried business travelers; enjoy well-lighted cocktail lounges; read business cards, menus and telephone dials better when they are printed in larger type; enjoy restaurants which serve decaffeinated coffee and more low-sodium items; and want chairs with arms on them and bathtubs with handholds and non-skid surfaces.

An example of a company which virtually entered the senior market by accident was Levi Strauss & Co. In 1983 Levi Strauss introduced Bend Over pants for women and Two-Horse Brand Jeans for men. The new entries were meant for the people in their 40s and 50s who liked the looks of traditional Levi products, but discovered their middle-age bodies did not fit the standard fabric cuts. The new products are looser, easier to fit, clean and wash. These attributes made them very popular with the over-60 segment. Another industry which is changing is the cosmetic industry which is gradually showing more advertisements with women in their 50s. The American Association of Retired Persons based in Washington, D.C., has a variety of discount programs for its 15 million members. These discounts are for such items as Avis, Hertz and National Car Rental Services; hotels operated by Sheraton, Travel Lodge, Holiday Inns and Best Western International; and even a prescription drug discount and group insurance plans.

If there is one commonality to which the health or consumer marketer is going to have to pay attention, it is the need to be sensitive to the unique characteristics of the mature person. In marketing their services or products it will be necessary to develop unique strategies related to select target groups. Marketers will require the use of sophisticated marketing tools. One of these strategy tools is POSITIONING.

POSITIONING STRATEGIES FOR LONG-TERM AND SENIOR CARE SERVICES

Interrelating Positions to the Marketing Mix

One of the basic concepts in marketing is the use of service differentiation by developing positions according to marketing mix strategies. In other words, positioning strategies can be developed according to the marketing mix components of: pricing, place, product and promotion characteristics.

PRICING COMPONENT

Selecting a pricing strategy for a specific long-term or senior care service is part of the positioning of the service in the minds of the providers and consumers within the community. The strategy's goal is to position the service to attract an adequate market share without also attracting a devastating competitive reaction. For example, some pricing strategies could be related to developing perceptions within the community of:

1. Are the services to be priced meant to be perceived as 'high-priced and high quality' or as 'low-priced and quantity-oriented' for easier access to care?
2. Depending upon the local reimbursement levels, are the services to be priced at a level related to limits on Medicare coverage or will there be a high co-payment?

The medical provider who refers clients to your services or the consumer who directly seeks services will develop an image or perception within their minds about how your services are priced. Medicare and Medicaid reimbursement levels will be very important to the consumer, and thus, will play an important role within the perception that is derived. In other words, think of how you would like the community to perceive your services' costs and fees.

PRODUCT COMPONENT

The product component of the marketing mix related to the physical characteristics of the service or the way in which it is delivered. In other words, how is my service unique or different from my competitors and how do I want my services perceived in the community as related to product characteristics? For example, some questions which describe product positioning are:

1. Are my services to be perceived as being general or specialized?
2. Are the services to be perceived as being available for all levels of mature adults or just select segments within the older population?
3. Are my services perceived as 'personal' or as 'factory-line' oriented by the older population within the community?
4. Are the services perceived as being of high quality or low quality?
5. Is the staff within my organization perceived as being helpful and courteous or disrespectful?
6. Do medical providers and discharge planners perceive our services and organization as highly professional and easy to work with or as difficult and unprofessional?

All of these positioning strategies are related to the actual service being provided or the organization in which the services operate. All quality of care, staff relations, procedures, cleanliness, and service are involved in positioning the service through the use of the product component of the marketing mix.

PLACE COMPONENT

The place component is a very important one as it relates to location, mode of delivery and access to care. These issues are very sensitive to an older population and can be very important in developing unique positions within the minds of the population. Some positioning strategy questions could be:

1. Are the services to be perceived as highly accessible or limited in accessibility?
2. Is the service to be perceived as flexible in hours in which service can be obtained?
3. Is the service perceived as a single office, clinic, group practice, institution, or even as a franchise?
4. Is the service to be perceived as one in which the patient has to go to obtain the service or does it have the flexibility of coming to the patient, if needed?
5. Is the perception of the service related to having easy access through public transportation or is a car required?
6. Is the service perceived as being in a safe location with adequate parking, lighting and security?
7. Is the perception of the service related to having to wait a considerable amount of time for an appointment?

All of these positioning strategies are important to the older population. These images and perceptions of the service dictate how and why people make referrals to your services.

PROMOTION COMPONENT

The promotion component of the marketing mix is related to how you communicate with the community; the purpose or mission of the existence of the organization; and the perception of how you market your services. Some promotion positioning questions are:

1. Are the materials used for promotion perceived as 'hard sell', 'soft sell', 'educational', or 'goodwill'?
2. Is the service perceived as 'serving the community' or just 'serving the financial need of the proprietors and providers'?
3. Is the service perceived as being highly thought of in terms of referrals by discharge planners, providers, other health professionals, or consumers?
4. Is the service widely known to the community or is it selectively known by a few segments of the marketplace?
5. Is the service perceived as being progressive in terms of provided services?
6. Is the organization perceived as being secretive or readily available to distribute needed information about the services or treatment procedures?

All of these place positioning strategies relate to the amounts, quality, and direction of the information communicated to the population by the organization.

The four components, or the four Ps, of the marketing mix can be a tremendous base to work from in developing positioning strategies. There is an old saying that, 'If all else fails, always fall back on the four Ps of the marketing mix for strategy development.'

HEAD-ON POSITIONING STRATEGY

Al Ries and Jack Trout in their book, *Positioning: The Battle For Your Mind,* state that, 'You can't compete head-on against a company that has a strong position. You can go around, under or over, but never head-on.' This statement describes the positioning aspect of 'not taking on' the strong competitor within a community or service marketplace. The direction was to take advantage of weaknesses or gaps within the marketplace. A great example of this trend is the HMO marketplace in Northern California. Kaiser's HMO dominates the marketplace, yet over twelve new HMOs have been developed during the last ten years. These new HMOs marketed themselves related to services not available through Kaiser; more personal care than Kaiser; better fees; etc. The new HMOs identified a niche in the marketplace and went after it in the minds of the consumers. Several of the new HMOs appear to be succeeding in battling for the remaining marketshare not 'owned' by Kaiser. Very few of the new HMOs have the financial base to compete with Kaiser on the same 'ground'. These new HMOs are trying to position themselves as being differentiated from Kaiser in terms of weaknesses within the Kaiser system or gaps in service delivery within the marketplace.

There is a new feeling the last few years that comparison marketing is a strong positioning strategy. The upsurge in comparison advertising in the media testifies to this trend. There appears to be much less hesitation in placing the new brand right alongside the entrenched market leader. However, the direct 'head-on' strategy against a market leader is risky. Positioning with an idea may provide a mechanism for head-on marketing. For example, the Vick Chemical Company positioned their cold remedy, Nyquil, with the idea of assuring a 'good night's sleep', rather than going head-on against the market leader in cold remedies. Most marketers would appraise this type of positioning strategy as applications of service differentiation or market segmentation rather than examples of new concepts.

POSITIONING WITH SOCIAL ACCOUNTABILITY

There is a major trend towards consumer protectionism. Being socially accountable for your products or services is becoming widely accepted by the population. The guarantee of consumer satisfaction by organizations is being stimulated by more distrust of consumer services/products by the population. This is especially true for the maturing segment of the population. The item mentioned earlier that it will be difficult to 'con' the maturing population is an important one for positioning. The creditability of long-term and senior care services must be enhanced in order to develop consumer 'faith' in your services. It is evident that health organizations will be faced with the difficult challenge of recognizing and dealing with the business conflicts of social responsibility to the client and organizational profitability.

'BEING FIRST' STRATEGY

In an overcommunicated marketplace positioning becomes an organized system for entering the consumer's mind. The easiest way into a person's mind is to be first. 'Imprinting' your new services into the minds of the consumer usually occurs only when the first encounter between a new service and consumer is initiated. We build loyalty for our services by getting there first and providing no reason for the consumer to ever switch to a competitor. There is an old saying that, 'It is better to be a big fish in a small pond rather than to be a small fish in a big pond.' History shows that the first product or service brand into the consumer's mind gets twice the long-term market share of the next best competitor. If your service is first into the marketplace it is important to communicate your market leadership as strongly and quickly as possible. The major reason that market leaders lose marketshare is change. It is important to constantly reinforce the positioning of your services and to keep your service current and quality-oriented.

An example of 'being first' for a positioning strategy is the new expansion into Life Care Services. Life Care is still a relatively new concept integrating the traditional services of a retirement community with the long-term health care found in a nursing home. There are more than 600 Life Care Communities throughout the United States. These Life Care Communities typically charge a residential entrance fee and monthly payment fees. Life time living accommodations typically total between $15,000 to over $100,000 with monthly service fees of $250 to $500. The services included for residents are: medical care, transportation, living quarters, meals, personal assistance, emergency assistance, funeral expenses, counseling, recreational activities, and continuing education classes. With the population maturing at such a fast rate these initial Life Care Communities may have successfully positioned themselves for the long-term.

POSITIONING IN A HIGHLY COMPETITIVE MARKETPLACE

The majority of the time it is not possible to be first into a marketplace. In most long-term and senior care service marketplaces there are numerous competitors providing similar services. The traditional positioning strategy in this case is to reposition the completion. In other words, in order to position a new service into the minds of consumers in saturated marketplaces, it is necessary to move the positioning of the competition out of the consumer's mind. In order for a repositioning strategy to be effective, there needs to be a message given that initiates the change to your service. However, just stating that your services are better than the competition is not a strong repositioning strategy. Traditionally, mentioning a competitor or comparing a competitor's service was considered highly unethical. Comparative positioning is not illegal. Performed honestly repositioning against one's competitors can be positive for the marketplace. It keeps the providers alert and responsive to the needs of the maturing population.

ATTACHMENT TO THE ORGANIZATION BY DEVELOPING A QUALITY NAME

Goodwill and brand loyalty are vitally important concepts in marketing health services. People tend to want to be 'attached' to a particular health service or provider over a period of time for security reasons. One of the most important positioning strategies related to attachment is developing a name for your service or organization. A crucial marketing decision for positioning is related to deriving a name which will be remembered by the marketplace. Health care services have historically been delinquent in deciding on marketing-related names for their services.

Developing a name for a service can be approached from various perspectives. First of all, a strong positioning name is one in which the customer/client relates to the type of service which is provided. For example, the MEALS ON WHEELS PROGRAM reflects a uniqueness and explains the basic service which is provided. A second approach is to keep the name simple yet find a unique 'marketing niche' for the name. For example, a local crisis telephone line in San Francisco is called the TALK LINE and the actual telephone number is a prefix followed by the four numbers associated with the letters TALK. A third perspective is to be creative and develop a 'catchy' name with a historical perspective, such as ON LOK SENIOR HEALTH SERVICES. All of these different approaches position the organization in the minds of the community. Other examples of well positioned names include such senior services as the GRAY PANTHERS, SENIOR ESCORT, SELF-HELP FOR THE ELDERLY, RETIREMENT JOBS, INC., GOLDEN GATE SENIOR SERVICES, and THE YMCA CHRISTMAS CAMP FOR SENIORS.

Sometimes a full name is not necessary as abbreviations become the positioning strategy. Think about our recognition of abbreviations such as HHS, ACHA, L-T-C, HUD, IBM, CARE, and AHA. They are a powerful positioning statement and highly recognizable.

POSITIONING SLOGANS AND LOGOS

An interesting concept in positioning products or services in health care is the use of slogans which represent these products/services. A slogan usually represents a 1) feeling we want to express about our service or 2) a key characteristic of the service. Slogans can be very stylish and creative. For example, a local preventive dental service is called Smile America and its slogan is 'Smile America is here to keep you smiling.' The slogan reflects the purpose of the preventive cleaning service and is also memorable. Another example would be a local wellness program which provides preventive programs for the mature population. Its slogan is 'Let's Work Together For Life'. The slogan reflects the purpose of the program and the importance of the cooperation between the providers of the program and the population they serve. Other slogans which are well positioned include Health Style Group's 'Helping People Help Themselves' in Illinois; Therapeutics Services, Inc.'s 'Advances in Diagnosis and Treatment' in Philadelphia; Busch & Associates' 'Your Competitive Edge' in Michigan; and St. Luke's Hospital of Kansas City's "100-A Century of Service/A Heritage of Excellence".

A position can also be established through the creative process of developing a logo. There are successful companies which just specialize in developing the most appropriate and potentially effective logo for a specific organization. A well-developed logo can position the long-term and senior care service in the minds of its consumers. One of the most successful logos and symbols in health care is the picture of the palms of two hands with a rainbow underneath representing United Way. Another successful symbol has been the Family Service Agency's symbol of two adults and two children within an oval parameter. Others include Blue Shield's medical insigna involving the staff of Aesculapius; Blue Cross' cross with an artist's sketch of a person in the middle with a circle around him; The Blood Center for Southwest Louisiana's two hearts on top of each other with one heart filled with blood dripping into the bottom heart; Adventist Health System-West's map of the United States marked off with the western states for territory they serve; and many different wellness programs with their derivative of a rising sun logo.

A fine example of the development of a new symbol and logo for positioning strategies is the logo Scott & White recently developed. Scott & White is an internationally-known clinic interrelated with Texas A & M University's College of Medicine in Temple, Texas. Scott & White is a hospital, clinic, research center, and educational center. The decision was made to refer to the whole medical complex as "Scott & White". This decision then made it necessary to create a symbol that would position "Scott & White" as a medical organization. From their news release it appears they started with Scott & White's Mission Statement of providing medicine, education and research and attempted to find a symbol which represented these three areas. They considered a cross, eternal flame and the staff of Aesculapius. The decision was made to use a derivative of the caduceus—the winged staff with two serpents that is the symbol of the U.S. Army Medical Corps. The designer created a symbol which incorporates the caduceus with the name Scott and White in the Garamond typeface. A modified version of the letters 'S' and 'W' were stylized with the medical symbol. From the market surveys it appears that the logo and symbol have been successful in developing the position desired—recognition that Scott & White is a medical organization whether the hospital, clinic, research center or educational center is involved. It has turned out to be a highly successful 'positioning strategy'.

POSITIONING IN SUMMARY

You can position anything from a person to an entire organization in the minds of the consumer/provider. The major difference in positioned a health product versus a service is the technique or strategy utilized. The most important influence in positioning a product is the visual and physical aspect of the product while a service is positioned mainly by verbal communication. As the article has outlined, communication is the most important tool related to positioning your services to the mature population. Positioning services requires some courage, risk-taking, vision for the future, adaptability to change, subtleness, patience, and a willingness to use marketing tools. Al Ries and Jack Trout outlined six basic questions that need to be answered in order to organize a positioning program. The questions are:

1. What current position do you own already in the minds of the providers/consumers in the marketplace? Some basic survey techniques can supply this kind of information.
2. What position do you want to own in the marketplace?
3. What competitors and competitive positions must you overcome or find a niche among them?
4. What are your financial resources to develop a position within the marketplace? It takes money to communicate and develop a position in the minds of the providers/consumers.
5. Can you stick to your marketing plan for developing a long-term position within the marketplace? Positioning is not a short-term activity. It takes time to build recognition, perception and loyalty to a service.

6. Do your positions truly match your organization's or staff's attributes? The position of the service must 'represent' the service. For example, if your position is related to the quality of care, your service better be of high quality.

There are a number of sound elements of marketing strategy embodied in the overall application of positioning. Using the concept of positioning can make your marketing program more meaningful and productive. Positioning is a concept which is cumulative. It takes into account a long-term development of your services. It can last the length of time your service exists.

Long-term and senior care administrators need to address the issues of rising demand for their services; restrictive reimbursement policies; an expanding, and in some ways, an already overcrowded market; and providers/clients who are overcommunicated with by many alternative services. POSITIONING the services available for mature sectors of our population in the minds of the providers and clients will become a key marketing tool during the remaining part of the century.

REFERENCES

Achenbaum, Alvin, 'Who Says You Need Research to Position A Brand?', *Journal of Advertising,* Vol. 3, Summer, 1974, p. 21-24.

Brody, Elaine, 'Women's Changing Roles: The Aged Family and Long Term Care for the Aging', *National Journal,* October 27, 1979.

Clabaugh, Maurice, 'A Marketing Orientation For The Nursing Home Industry', *Journal of Health Care Marketing,* Vol. 2, No. 2, 1982, p. 7-14.

Feldstein, Paul, *Health Economics,* John Wiley & Sons, New York, 2nd Edition, 1983.

Foundation of the American College of Health Care Administration, 'Working to Improve the Delivery of Long-term Health Care', Maryland, ACHCA, 1982.

Maggard, John, 'Positioning Revisited', *Journal of Marketing,* January, 1976, p. 63-66.

Pound, Leslie, 'A Major Wrinkle In American Life', *San Francisco Chronicle,* September 11, 1983, p. A13.

Ries, Al and Trout, Jack, *Positioning: The Battle For Your Mind,* Warner Books, New York, 1981.

Ries, Al and Trout, Jack, 'The Positioning Era Cometh', *Advertising Age,* April, 1972, p. 35-38.

Scott & White, *News Release,* July 21st, 1983, Texas A & M University, Temple, Texas.

U.S. Dept. of Census. *America In Transition: An Aging Society,* Washington, U.S. Printing Office, 1983.

Vogel, Ronald, *Long-term Care: Perspectives From Research and Demonostrations,* HFMA, Dept. of HHS, 1983.

Weissert, William. 'Long-term Care: An Overview', *Health United States, 1978,* Washington, U.S. Printing Office.

PRESS RELEASE

"IMPLEMENTING DRGs: DEVELOPING EFFECTIVE STRATEGIES"
(Based on the FINAL 1984 REGULATIONS)

Videotape 35 minutes
Produced January, 1984

Practical legal viewpoints and ideas are presented by three noted health care attorneys specializing in regulatory matters. The participants include: Norman P. Jeddeloh, Legal Counsel to the University of Illinois at Chicago; Jack R. Bierig, Partner, Sidley & Austin, Chicago; and Henry S. Allen, Jr., Partner, Allen & Reed, Chicago. Also, the program features David Palmer, the HCFA attorney responsible for drafting the DRG regulations. Mr. Palmer offers technical assistance based upon his knowledge of the regulations.

This presentation is based upon the final regulations published January 1, 1984. It identifies frequently occurring issues the hospital will face under the DRG system. Among other topics, it explores and analyzes patient transfers, outliers, cost reimbursement, DRG #468-470, rebundling, and similar issues. Its objective is to help the hospital develop proper procedures and strategies that will assure maximum DRG payments. A number of practical techniques are offered for prospering within the system. Appeal mechanisms for challenging unfavorable decisions are presented.

The program content is directed to hospital administrators, hospital counsel, trustees, financial officers and other key hospital professionals including physicians in charge of clinical management.

The videotape is approximately 35 minutes in length, and available for purchase only, on 3/4" or 1/2" format, at a cost of $300.00, through the Center for Educational Development, 833 S. Wood Street, Chicago, Illinois 60612, (312) 996-7912.

Challenges in Marketing Mental Health Senior Services

Sharon George

INTRODUCTION

Marketing is an idea whose time has come in mental health service delivery. In any gathering of mental health planners or administrators marketing jargon is bandied about as frustrated service deliverers seek answers to the dilemma posed by growing demand and shrinking resources. The new buzz words are "packaging, selling, and promoting". As frustration increases, the grabbing at straws of jargon and half-understood concepts accelerates, but with little apparent benefit.

This paper will first explore the challenge and the opportunities for mental health planners and administrators to understand and use a marketing approach to management. Then it will consider the challenge to use that understanding of marketing to reduce fear and misunderstanding of mental illness and increase support for mental health services.

THE FIRST CHALLENGE

Since administrators operate daily amid fiscal crises and mutually exclusive demands, it is understandable that they are quick to grab straws of marketing. Yet the challenge is to slow down in the midst of the storm long enough to get a look at the whole concept. Market-

---

Sharon George is Executive Director, Mental Health Association of San Francisco, S.F., CA; organizer of the San Francisco Self-Help Clearinghouse and other self-help groups in Texas.

69

ing, according to Kotler, is "a management orientation that holds that the key task of the organization is to determine needs and wants of target markets and to *adapt* the organization to delivering the desired satisfactions more effectively and efficiently than its competition in a way that preserves or enhances the consumers' and societies' well-being."[1] Application of the marketing concept requires systematic identification of target markets, any present or potential consumers, and thoughtful analysis of the needs and desires of each in terms of what the organization has to give or exchange. Then, those groups or organizations in society, such as legislators or the media, that have a potential or present impact on the organization must be identified. The interests and concerns of these people must be assessed, too, as they comprise the environment in which the organization must operate. Finally, a comprehensive plan based on systematic data collection and analysis is designed to deliver services to selected targets through appropriate means, in a way that is compatible with the environment.

Marketers then, use a variety of strategies and tactics to implement their plans. Packaging design and distribution channels are plan elements as are promotion and public relations techniques, advertising, and selling. Because the planning and analysis phase—the "real work" of marketing—is largely unseen, mental health administrators have a tendency to confuse the plan elements with the whole. And because they are harried, they are impatient and vulnerable to looking for quick fixes.

Kotler notes that non-profit service systems, including public, tax supported services, are usually product or service oriented. Then when support begins to decline, they "resort" to selling. Only later, do they realize the need to define their target markets more carefully, to research their needs, wants, and values and to *adapt* the services to meet those needs (offering people what they want rather than what we think they want) and to communicate more effectively. Only then do they market their services.[2]

Mental health planners and administrators are beginning to resort to selling as evidenced by their eager grabbing of marketing jargon and techniques. Even the term "marketing", as commonly used, is synonymous with selling. They can ill afford the time and further loss of support that will likely result, before they too, get the mes-

---

[1]Kotler, p. 35
[2]Kotler, p. 33

sage and learn to market. I believe the digression is unnecessary and that they can learn from the mistakes of earlier efforts. They can discipline themselves to go through the process of rethinking, refocusing, and reorganizing to rebuild support that will carry into the future. Simple? Yes. Easy? No. Can it be done? If there's a willingness, yes. If not, . . .

THE SECOND CHALLENGE

The dominant response to consideration of mental illness is fear. Preliminary results of a program to induce management in industry to include psychiatric coverage in insurance programs indicates that managers are reluctant and anxious about discussing mental illness even in the context of insurance. Services for those with mental illness are called "mental health services" as if to obscure the fact that what is treated is illness. There is a rationale to justify this name game. One wonders why the Cancer Society is not similarly known as the "Uncancer Society"? Mental illness is discussed in whispers, and we may never tell even our closest friends when a family member suffers from mental illness.

The author had the opportunity to attend a national conference on the stigma that accompanies mental illness. Leaders from NIMH, from Mental Health Associations, union leaders, business and government leaders were there to discuss and design strategies to reduce stigma. On the afternoon of the second day the meeting was interrupted when a mentally ill woman walked to the front of the room and began to speak. What she said was unremarkable. What her audience did was astonishing. Two hundred "leaders" in the movement to reduce stigma stared straight ahead, embarrassed, and uncomfortable. When she finished, no one acknowledged her presence, and the speaker immediately resumed his talk.

Attempts to reduce fear and apprehension have been sporadic and largely unsuccessful. Funding for traditional mental health education programs has always been limited and was the first to be cut. The challenge planners and administrators face is to build on our marketing approach and apply marketing strategies and tactics to build support and understanding for the mentally ill.

Four areas will be considered: Product definition, demystification, dispelling myths, removing barriers. These objectives are not mutually exclusive or disjointed. Progress toward any of them will be progress toward each of the others and to the goals of removing fear.

PRODUCT DEFINITION

Who do mental health planners and administrators serve? What do they provide? Answers to those questions are as varied as the people who answer them and tend to be framed in terms of specific services and programs. Just as banks are "institutions designed to meet changing and varied financial needs of their customers",[3] so mental health services are more than therapy groups, or clinics, or community re-entry programs.

The first step to clear definition of the product is to delineate target markets. Our market, largely for public services, is comprised of the 1% of our population with a schizophrenic illness and the one-half to 1% with a manic-depressive illness or some other form of brain anomaly. We know little about the causes of these illnesses nor do we know how to cure them. We do know some ways to reduce suffering, to improve levels of functioning, and to enhance the quality of the lives their victims lead.

Another market is those who are called by E. Fuller Torrey, "the worried well".[4] These people can also be described as having adjustment or living problems severe enough to require assistance. They may be considered as ill as a result of emotional disequilibrium, much as a person with fluid on the lungs is ill from physical disequilibrium. There are estimated to be 5% of our population in need of treatment at any one time and all of us are at risk of requiring such care. In fact, one out of eight of us, will be treated at some point in our lives. We know more about treatment for these people and most get well or have equilibrium restored or become less worried.

What is important is to distinguish clearly between the two populations and make realistic assessments of what can be done.

In the broadest sense then, the product at hand is reduction of suffering for the mentally ill, reduction in the distress to society caused by mental illness and improved quality of life for the mentally ill and

---

[3]Kotler, p. 12
[4]Torrey, p. 225

their families. All planners and administrators need to say what they can do, do what they say, and communicate both in ways and places where they can be heard. That is marketing.

DEMYSTIFICATION

The next objective is to demystify mental illness, its treatment and mental health professionals. Interestingly, even the language mental health professionals use is metaphorical. They speak of "breaking up" and "breaking down". They are frequently trained to be obscure and non-intrusive. They have been so distressed by the behavior of mentally ill people that they are reluctant to discuss themselves, their work or its impact on them. Taken together and in the context of fear and shame it all seems a great mystery.

Yet there is neither magic nor black magic involved in mental illness or its treatment. The experiences of great sadness or euphoria are easily described. Torrey[5] does a good job of quoting patients with schizophrenia to describe and illustrate their altered sensory perceptions, inability to concentrate and other experiences common to schizophrenia. Treatment techniques can be described with similar ease: certain medications have certain effects and limitations. Hospitalization is necessary under certain circumstances, community care is better under others. Then, mental health professionals are not really mind readers after all; they are just people with particular forms of training in sets of skills anyone could learn. They have families and earn livings like everyone else.

Once again, the issue becomes communication in ways and places where the message can be heard. The emphasis here is on *places.* Mental health professionals need to go where their target markets are if they want them to hear what is said. As one person commented, "We only hear what we need at the moment we need it, so the challenge is to have the message out there at the exact moment—at each exact moment of need". Another creative person suggested that there be shopping mall drop-in centers for people with problems. It is an interesting notion that needs further consideration. As a component of a comprehensive marketing plan, that, too, is marketing.

---

[5]Torrey, Chap. 2, pp. 5-38.

DISPEL MYTHS

Myths concerning the origins of mental illness have existed at least since some Biblical thinker pondered the question, "Who sinned, this man or his parents?". And society has been seeking to assign blame just as long. Those afflicted with mental illness and their families continue to carry a double burden: the burden of illness and the burden of guilt.

All illness and human suffering were once considered retribution for evil while prosperity was considered reward for virtue. During the past several hundred years that has changed as society has recognized the causes of social and physical misfortune. Gradually, we have accepted a responsibility to provide for the poor, physically and developmentally disabled, older people. While more needs to be done, there is fundamental agreement that these are people who deserve to be cared for and treated with sympathy and compassion.

Society has not accepted responsibility for people with mental illness in the same way. Service provision, where services exist, is often contingent on some implicit promise on the part of recipients to get better. It seems strange that society requires a mental patient to be prepared to work or support himself or to live independently after a month or a year, yet it does not require a blind person to promise to see before he is offered support in his daily life. Not knowing how to cure the illness, we, in effect, blame the patient. Part of the problem has to do with myths about origins of illness; part is because mental health professionals do not clearly define their target market so they respond to the person with the schizophrenia in the same way they might respond to one with an illness of dis-equilibrium or one of the worried well. Either way, this is a marketing problem that can be addressed in a marketing framework.

Other myths are that all problems of living are appropriate mental health issues, followed by responding myths that say mental health services are so broad they defy boundaries and are so big, they cannot be dealt with. A further and more destructive myth holds that mental patients are violent and to be feared. In an attempt to deal humanly with mental patients who did become violent, the legal system created the defense of "not guilty by reason of insanity". Without debating the merits of the defense, it is clear that a backlash has followed, using the unfortunate line of reasoning, "If some people with mental illness are violent, then all people with mental illness are dangerous".

Still other myths exist but these are enough to illustrate the point that accurate, concise information needs to be communicated in ways and places and at times that people can hear them and respond.

REMOVE BARRIERS

Barriers to treatment take several forms. Persons in need may not know where to go or how to tell when they need help. They may resist because of fear and shame or because of pressure from family or culture. The lack of clarity about who mental health professionals serve, and how, combined with the public's unrealistic expectations and fears have contributed to the reduction of public support for services.

Then, when a person does seek mental health services further barriers are erected. Reintegration into the community, housing, employment, and social relationships are all hampered or made impossible by the fears of mental illness. A corporate employment representative pointed out that there are two kinds of disabilities: intrinsic disabilities which are directly and logically related to a physical condition. A person without legs will not run far. Then there are imposed disabilities—imposed because of fear and misunderstanding. Even with legs that person will not run far if he is shackled. So, once again, mental patients suffer twice. They suffer the effects of their illnesses and whatever intrinsic disabilities arise, and they suffer disabilities imposed upon them.

Mental health professionals have been only mildly successful in their attempts to remove those barriers, given their present state of unclarity and mystery. The same accurate, clear information disseminated in ways and places and times that people can hear them will go far to eliminate the barriers to treatment and to reintegration.

Two challenges have been presented. The first is a challenge to mental health planners and administrators to adopt a new way of doing what they do through a comprehensive marketing approach to management of mental health services. It is also a challenge to avoid the pitfalls of looking for a quick "selling" fix. The second challenge is to use marketing strategies to confront those fundamental questions of definition and communication in the context of that new approach. What the mental health planners and administrators have done has not brought enough clarity, reduced the shroud of mystery enough, dispelled myths enough or broken enough barriers of resistance.

There is no evidence that doing more of the same will produce the desired results, nor that it will prevent the further erosion of services. There is evidence that other non-profit systems have benefited greatly from a marketing approach, and that other health care systems are benefiting from such an approach. Based on the evidence, the two challenges become one: Are we willing to risk change for greater gain or will we continue as we are?

BIBLIOGRAPHY

Kotler, Philip, MARKETING MANAGEMENT: 4th Ed., Prentice-Hall, Inc., Englewood Cliffs, New Jersey 07632, 1980.
Torrey, E. Fuller, SURVIVING SCHIZOPHRENIA, A FAMILY MANUAL, Harper & Row, Publishers, New York, N.Y. 1983.

Skilled Nursing Facility Marketing: A *Better* Piece of Pie

Matthew Midgett

As America's senior population continues to grow, so does the demand for senior-related services.

Currently in this country, one out of every eleven people is a "senior citizen." Within 50 years seniors will account for almost a quarter of the population.

In response to this trend, providers of many services including financial, recreational and medical, scramble to acquire their share of this growing market. At least one industry has a guaranteed clientele: U.S. Census Bureau statistics currently list over 19,000 long-term health care facilities nationwide. With approximately five percent of Americans over age 65 requiring nursing home care, nearly all such facilities have significant waiting lists.

Even with the emergence of senior care alternatives such as home health and adult day-care, skilled nursing facilities enjoy a "patient base" no longer available to most acute hospitals and other health care providers.

Given the assurance of "census success," what marketing techniques could possibly be of interest to long-term/senior care administrators?

Richard Hebbel, former Nursing Home Association President, delegate to the White House Conference on Aging, and second-generation nursing home administrator, cites the need to look at more than just the numbers. Says Hebbel, "Despite the appearance of assured success, many factors affect the profitability of long-term

---

Matthew Midgett is an Account Executive, J. Pinto & Associates, a marketing communications firm in San Diego, CA.

health care facilities. Government regulations, the type of facility and services offered, and perhaps most importantly, sources of payment, all determine the ability to succeed in this business. Careful marketing can maximize each of these factors.''

But wait a minute! If the number of seniors requiring long-term care is on the rise, and waiting lists continue to grow, why the need for ''marketing''?

Despite full census', a survey of successful nursing home administrators shows that they recognize a need to attract not only government-subsidized applicants, whose flat rate charges allowable by law provide only minimal profits at best—but the more profitable private pay patient as well.

By carefully proportioning the number of subsidized and private pay patients, nursing homes can provide better accomodations and services for both.

Since most facilities run at full or near full capacity, this proportion of ''patient mix'' is crucial to fiscal advance.

For skilled nursing homes, which offer around-the-clock care to patients who are unable to care for themselves, maintaining census is accomplished in an almost singular manner. According to Hebbel, the decision to admit a person to a skilled nursing or convalescent home is most often made at the acute hospital level.

''People don't look ahead to the need for nursing home care. As a last minute decision after having been notified that the patient can't return home, the personal physician and hospital discharge planner frequently are called upon to advise the family on the preferred facility.''

Common marketing techniques, including paid advertising and media coverage, aren't effective in reaching these important people. A more aggressive, direct approach is needed: personalized correspondence, community involvement programs, open houses, and in-house publications all help to familiarize local referral parties with the facility.

Says John Pinto, president of J. Pinto & Associates, a San Diego firm specializing in health care clients, ''A 'birddogging' system of contact and follow-up with key people can greatly enhance future referrals. Establishing a file of local physicians and discharge planners—who they are, their interests, previous referrals and other information—can keep your name before the right people when the decisions are made.''

Adds Mel Stuart, senior associate in the firm and former administrator of New York's Bellevue Hospital, "It is vitally important that a skilled nursing facility administrator keep his vision clear, his goals in mind . . . and within reach. The marketing plan should be a logical step-by-step approach to realistic goals. All the factors contributing to referrals must be considered in a prioritized manner."

One important qualification for referral, location is often a criteria for recommending a skilled nursing home. Explains Hebbel, "With patients requiring regular medical attention, physicians often will visit only a limited number of facilities, usually very close to a hospital or medical office complex. However, there are exceptions—an excellent reputation will attract patients nearly anywhere."

Obviously patient care, visibility and overall image are all points which administrators recognize as essential to success.

Staffing and staff attitudes, another prevalent concern of administrators, can be influenced by traditional techniques.

Competition for qualified personnel is great, and word of staff problems and their effect on the facility often precede any positive report to prospective patients and their families. And since nursing and dietary staff members often interface with important referral sources—physicians—they can have direct bearing on the success of any marketing efforts.

As with patient referral sources, personnel agents specializing in nursing home clients must be courted to provide preferred applicants.

One key to establishing loyalty among existing staff is personal pride in the institution. Frequent and sincere praise can work wonders—as can positive incentives and a sense of involvement with administration. Says a nurse who has worked in nursing homes for over 20 years, the last eight of which at the same facility, "I feel that my experience, knowledge and ideas have some worth here. When I make a suggestion, someone listens. The patients know that their concerns will be considered. Some places make you feel like you're all victims of some distant dictator."

Maintaining such high standards in order to attract the more profitable private pay patient is expensive—and the profit margin at most facilities is small—generally less than a five percent return on revenue. Trapped in a vicious circle of having to provide expensive services in order to attract profitable patients to pay for them, administrators will continue to be challenged to capture a larger share of this "preferred clientele." Yet most administrators find the effort worthwhile. States Hebbel, "In the final analysis, we only benefit if the patient does. By providing better care for our patients, we in turn attract the kind of patient we need to maintain our standards."

A CASE IN POINT

How can skilled nursing facilities (SNF) administrators cut a better piece of the private pay pie?

How about adopting programs already proven successful by a so called "luxury liner" facility?

Designed and built two and one-half years ago with the needs and tastes of private pay patients in mind, Rancho Bernardo Convalescent Hospital has excelled in just what it set out to do: out class the competition, thus increasing the percentage of private pay patients to an enviable seventy percent. Remarks the innovative administrator, Ann Marie Smith, "Our fees are relatively high, but our patients and their families are accustomed to certain standards—and expect to have them maintained."

Many of these "standards" were built in: the hospital offers beautiful surroundings and well-designed treatment/therapy areas.

But aside from the superior accommodations, this hospital set out to win its elite clientele in other ways as well. Says Mrs. Smith, "We don't treat patients here, we treat *families.*" Likewise they not only seek the support of the usual referral sources, but have devoted most marketing efforts to gaining extensive community support. Mrs. Smith comments, "You must reach out to the immediate community if you expect their support. We went from zero patients on opening day to full census seven months later—the result of sticking to our high standards and giving of ourselves to the community."

The hospital's "community outreach" programs include:

- Making available meeting rooms at the hospital without fee to local civic groups and business firms.
- Participation in the Adopt-a-School program which offers high school course credits to those students visiting the hospital for hands-on geriatric experience.
- Purchasing books and magazine subscriptions as ongoing gifts to local libraries.
- Hosting a wheelchair Olympics attracting participants from throughout the area.
- Inviting the community and patients to view free, first-run movies as a regularly scheduled program at the hospital.

—Providing free holiday meals by invitation to local seniors living alone.

The hospital has found holidays to be a particularly effective time to bring patients and members of the community together. At Halloween, the facility became a "safe and sane" place for over 1,000 local children to trick-or-treat and watch spooky movies. An Octoberfest celebration featured food and gift booths manned by patients and staff, with proceeds used to provide car seats to parents unable to afford them for their children. To acknowledge St. Valentine's Day, over 1,000 helium-filled balloons were set free, sending self-addressed, stamped postcards as far away as central Mexico. Explains Mrs. Smith, "You can't imagine the joy those cards brought our patients, as their cards were returned from far and wide. But we really should have notified the FAA!"

Christmas is an especially busy time. Events are planned for staff as well as patients, and various religious services are held. Patients assemble food baskets to distribute to the needy, and the hospital sponsors a Toys for Tots collection drive.

Individually, the events don't require great amounts of either money or time. However, the positive image of the hospital they convey to the community is invaluable.

"We're a team here," says Mrs. Smith, "I think our success is due to the pride we take in our hospital 'family'. Both staff and patients feel a part of the 'outside' community. By participating in activities which provide community interaction, our patients benefit tremendously. And we become the preferred facility in the minds of people who perhaps someday will refer a family member, or choose us for themselves."

Control of the Marketing Effort in Health Care Organizations

James D. Suver, D.B.A.
John A. Miller, D.B.A.
Leonard Farr, M.H.A.

PREFACE

The long term care administrator is frequently confronted with poor publicity on the quality of health care provided to clients in nursing facilities. Many of these press releases are caused by lack of understanding on the part of the writer but in some cases, they are merely designed to create attention or sensationalism. An effective local public relations program can do much to alleviate the national, blanket approach by many studies. In addition, the providing of educational information can do much to further community goals in providing quality health. The approaches illustrated in this article offer some appropriate alternatives to the long term care administrator to make her organization more effective in coping with today's environment.

James D. Suver is Professor of Health Policy and Administration, School of Public Health, University of North Carolina at Chapel Hill; co-author of 3 books on Health Financial Management; Director of Masters Program, Department of Health Policy and Administration.

John A. Miller is Resident Dean and Professor of Marketing, College of Business and Management, University of Colorado, Colorado Springs; author of numerous marketing articles; and faculty member for the Hospital Financial Management Association's Annual National Institutes.

Leonard "Al" Farr is President and Chief Executive Officer of Saint Francis Hospital Systems, Colorado Springs, Colorado. He received his Bachelor of Science in Zoology from Louisiana State University, Baton Rouge, and Masters of Health Care Administration from Washington University, Saint Louis. He is very active in the Colorado Hospital Association and is currently serving as Chairman of the CHA Board of Directors. He also serves on various community boards and committees, including Silver Key, Better Business Bureau, and Salvation Army Advisory Board.

INTRODUCTION

The increasing emphasis on marketing activities by health care organizations poses new challenges to the health care administrator. Basically, these challenges fall into two areas.

1. Determining whether the marketing program has achieved the desired objectives. This could be considered to be an effectiveness goal.
2. Maximizing the benefits achieved from the resources used. This could be considered to be an efficiency goal.

Both of these goals need to be achieved if the marketing effort is to be successful and controlled. Measuring the achievement of the first goal, effectiveness, depends primarily on the proper setting of objectives. Measuring the achievement of the latter, efficiency, depends on the identification of output, and the proper use of accounting information.

The first section of this paper will concentrate on accomplishing the ''effectiveness'' function with emphasis on actual situations. The second section will build on the concepts in the first part and focus on techniques that can be used to measure the ''efficiency'' function. It is in this area that management needs to improve its control of the marketing effort.

THE IMPORTANCE OF IDENTIFYING MEASURABLE OBJECTIVES

When distilled to its essence, the ''control process'' is simply a matching of desired performance against actual performance, and it may involve specifying and taking corrective action to bring the two into line. Objectives are statements about what activities and performance levels are desired. Without clear, measurable, recorded statements which summarize desired activities, achievements, and performance levels, the control process lacks the necessary standards against which one evaluates actual activities and performance. Besides serving as a comparison point for evaluation purposes, objectives also serve at least two other functions: they give direction and they serve as incentive targets. Objectives offer direction to employees by publicly stating in what direction the organization should be heading. Should effort be directed toward increasing patients, or reducing costs . . . ? Objectives provide direction for choosing alternative strategies and courses of action. In addition, objectives or goals provide a target toward which the organization, departments, or employees may strive. Thus, they serve an incentive capacity—they are "something to shoot for." Objectives, therefore, while serving as standards of performance, can also give direction to and stimulate effort.

Control of the marketing effort presents a management challenge because of the general lack of adequate output measurement factors. A marketing program could be expected to achieve certain objectives such as an increase in total revenue, an improvement in community health, and/or favorable public opinion of the institution. Except for the objective to increase total revenue, adequate output indices do not generally exist for measuring output accomplishment objectives. It is even difficult to isolate just what proportion of increases in revenue might be related to specific marketing expenditures. The amount to be expended to achieve the marketing objectives, at best, becomes an educated guess under most circumstances. Well designed objectives are vital as the first step in controlling the marketing effort.

Characteristics of "Good" Objectives

Good objectives satisfy several criteria. They should be written, quantifiable, specific, achievable, and use "bench marks." Unless they are recorded in writing, objectives can be too easily lost, forgotten, misinterpreted, and overlooked. Objectives should be part of a written planning/control document which can be cited and used by the parties whose work is being assessed. Good objectives are quantified. Too often, broad unquantified generalizations are used in objectives. "To improve our institution's image" is a worthwhile direction, but how does one evaluate if or how well that objective has been achieved? Quantified goals which include numbers, percentages, ratios and the like can serve as evaluation points. With quantification one can tell whether or not, as well as to what extent, objectives have been reached.

Closely related to quantification is specificity. Good objectives are specific. A medical clinic in a college town may wish "to serve young people" . . . but what is young? While George Burns may wish that he were 18 again, to him 65 is young. Specific measurable characteristics—"males and females 13-34"—are part of well defined usable objectives.

Because objectives serve both an incentive function and an evaluative function it is very important that they be achievable. If objectives are set unrealistically too high, employees will "give up" and won't even try to reach them. They also will not accept them as fair standards against which their performance is compared. Conversely, too low objectives stimulate no improvements or higher performance levels, even though many, if not most, employees may not be troubled by having them used as "grading" or performance criteria levels.

Finally, good objectives include their own reference points or "bench marks" as bases for comparisons. A good objective doesn't merely suggest the desire "To increase Drug Clinic Program usage by 10%." Rather it includes the current "bench mark" level on which the improvement is to be made: "To increase Drug Clinic Program usage by 10% over current year's number of 600 clients served."

Types of Marketing Objectives

In the sphere of marketing responsibility and activity, objectives can be classified generally into two major categories—revenue-type objectives and communications-type objectives.

Revenue-Type Objectives. The first category includes objectives that are essentially revenue or revenue-related measures. Dollar revenue, unit revenue, market share, or revenue growth are clear examples. Similarly, cost per unit, reductions in costs, bed or room occupancy rates, service use rates and the like fall into this category as well.

Communication-Type Objectives. Too often managers focus their attention—often unfairly—on revenue-type objectives for marketing and neglect the development of communications-type objectives. Communications-type objectives generally are achievable through marketing communication and promotion activities. Examples include "first brand awareness" measures, measures of extent of knowledge, of preference rankings for the brand, product, or institution, and the like.

In some cases, marketing performance is assessed strictly on a "bottom line" profit level or revenue level performance criterion—a revenue-type objective. Yet, it is possible that factors outside the control of marketing—economic situation, technological factors, political/legal factors, socio/cultural characteristics—may be "at fault" for the discrepancies between desired and actual performance levels. If one is setting promotion objectives, this problem becomes significantly more acute. To measure an advertising campaign's effectiveness by evaluating revenue results may improperly totally ignore the effects of other marketing mix elements—such as product or service quality, product characteristics, price level, product or service availability, quality and extent of personal selling efforts—as well as of the previously mentioned factors outside the control of marketing.

EXAMPLES OF SPECIFIC MARKETING OBJECTIVES

Revenue-Type Objectives

1. During fiscal year 1982, to increase market share from current 30% of total metro hospital beds occupied to 35% of those occupied.
2. By year end 1982, to increase Cancer Pavilion bed occupancy rate from current 85% level to 90% level through expanded diagnosis program.
3. By end of fiscal 1982, to increase current 17% profitability level to 19%.
4. By year end 1982, to increase use of Outpatient Department from 3,685 visits (1981) to 4,000 visits through the Physician Education program.
5. etc.

Communication-Type Objectives

1. To increase unaided awareness of Metropolitan Hospital's Birthing Room from current level of 15% of metro area females ages 13 to 34 to 30% by August 1, 1983.
2. To increase knowledge of Barney Hospital's Spouse Live-In Recuperative Tower option from 10% to 20%, among metro area adults by year end 1982.
3. To increase "first preference ranking" for County General among metro area hospitals from 20% to 30% among 18 to 45-year-old county residents by end of fiscal 1982.
4. To establish image of Parker Memorial Hospital as the top-quality health care facility in the Smithville SMSA as measured among employed 18 to 65-year-olds by end of 1981 Image Campaign (no bench marks).
5. etc.

Other Types of Objectives

1. To develop four new significant In-Patient services during 1982.
2. To improve service to the Primary Service Area by expansion of free Elder Care information programs from 0-1 per month during 1982.

It is important to others that the objectives be as specific as possible if adequate control of the marketing effort is to be achieved.

SOME EXAMPLES OF MARKETING PROGRAMS IN WHICH THE OBJECTIVES WERE CLEARLY STATED AND OUTPUTS CLEARLY IDENTIFIED

By the middle 1970s, St. Francis Hospital in Colorado Springs was a health care service institution which was suffering from poor "positioning" and tight cash flow. In fact, in 1975 and 1976 the hospital operated in the red and was losing its patient base. The new CEO who arrived in March 1978 learned of two "strengths" of the hospital: first, the medical community felt that St. Francis had very good emergency rooms; second, a limited segment of the metro area population felt that St. Francis had an advantage in its good nursing care. Unfortunately, tight control by a previously overly conservative top management had resulted in a shortage of the most up-to-date equipment in the laboratory, radiology, and operating rooms. Further, a portion of the Colorado Springs populace—especially business people—". . . heard that St. Francis was having financial problems."

The New CEO at St. Francis decided to improve its position by building on its quality strengths and informing the community of those strengths. Prior to March 1978, St. Francis held third place among the three major Colorado Springs hospitals in several areas. For example, it had not been investing in up-to-date, sophisticated equipment, its pay for the nursing staff was lower by 50¢ an hour than either of the other two leading hospitals, and its delivery room usage also was lowest of the three. Beginning in spring 1978, as part of an overall longer-term marketing plan to upgrade St. Francis Hospital's image and position, to increase revenues and to improve profitability, top management at St. Francis established several marketing objectives and designed and implemented strategies and tactics to achieve those marketing objectives. Following are just a few examples of several objective/strategy/tactics/results examples from the four year period, spring 1978 through spring 1982.

AN EXAMPLE OF REVENUE-TYPE OBJECTIVES

The Alternative Birthing Center

The Problem/Opportunity

One problem facing St. Francis was that although its obstetrics/gynecology staff was highly qualified, its delivery room had a capacity for greatly increased usage.

Objectives

—To increase the number of deliveries rank of St. Francis from third to second of the three Colorado Springs hospitals;

—To make the community more aware of St. Francis' quality care and new service leadership.

Strategy

—To develop and provide an alternative birthing center/birthing room service;

—To publicize the new service to the community.

—To offer a new patient-oriented delivery system already in use in several other areas of the United States;

The Program

—Establish a birthing room/alternative birthing center facility;

—Publicize the birthing center through advertisements in newspapers, on TV and radio;

—Develop a package price for delivery which includes a free at-home visit by the RN team after the patient's discharge.

—To offer a new patient-oriented delivery system already in use in several other areas of the United States;

Results

—St. Francis is now clearly in strong second place according to number of deliveries of the three Colorado Springs hospitals;

—St. Francis' image was improved as a progressive hospital offering up-to-date, patient-oriented new services.

AN EXAMPLE OF COMMUNICATION-TYPE OBJECTIVES

The "Quality Plus" Money-Back Guarantee Program

The Problem/Opportunity

St. Francis had a strength in "quality of care" according to a medical technician resident who had had an opportunity to compare St. Francis with several other U.S. hospitals. A "money-back" satisfaction guaranteed program could serve to reassure patients and to publicize the quality of St. Francis and the confidence its medical and administrative staff had in its services.

Objectives

—To increase visibility in the community;
—To publicize the high quality of care available from St. Francis;
—To gain a competitive "positioning" edge by offering a unique service first in the Colorado Springs metro area.

Strategy

Develop and publicize a "satisfaction guaranteed or your money back" program for patients of St. Francis Hospital.

The Program

—Set aside $10,000 contingency to cover potential claims by patients;
—Publicize the "Quality Plus" guarantee service through full-page ads in local newspapers as well as in other media.
—Establish a mechanism within the hospital to implement the program.

Results

After the first year's existence of the program, a total of $2,300 had been "refunded" to patients under the Quality Plus guarantee (about 40% of the payments were for items lost—such as eyeglasses, etc.), on gross hospital revenues of about $24 million! The remaining $7,700 of the $10,000 originally put in reserve for the guarantee was returned as small bonuses to the 656 hospital employees, about a $12.38 "tip" incentive/reward for their part in assuring patient satisfaction during the first year of the Quality Plus program.

AN EXAMPLE OF OTHER TYPES OF OBJECTIVES

"Express Admission" Program

The Problem/Opportunity

St. Francis served a significant number of older patients in its neighborhood who tended to use hospital facilities on a fairly repetitive routine basis. Frequent "check-ins" required time from staff and patients for gathering necessary information. There was an opportunity to offer a new benefit by streamlining repeat check-in procedures and to gain a "position/image" advantage by being first to offer another new service in the community.

Objectives

—To develop a streamlined, time-efficient hospital check-in procedure for repeat or returning patients;
—To gain visibility and enhancement of a positive "leader" image through the publicizing of the new service.

The Program

—Develop and implement distribution of an "Express Admission Card," like a plastic credit card, for staff, current patients, and the general community;
—Publicize the "Express Admission Card" program;
—Distribute cards to staff and current patients;
—Use advertisements in newspapers with coupons which offered Express Admission Cards to people in the community who desired them;
—Using direct mail, offer cards to businesses as a service to their employees.

Results

—Approximately 2,000 cards have been distributed in the Colorado Springs metro area;
—The average admission time for the typical outpatient admit now runs about 3-4 minutes, compared to 20 minutes before implementation of the Express Admission Card program;
—Information and records accuracy have been improved significantly;
—The hospital has gained another opportunity to publicize a service "first" in the community;

—Elderly patients especially appreciate the ease of repeat check-in without the hassles of providing detailed but necessary information already on file.

Other Examples

The list of examples from St. Francis Hospital could be expanded to include such programs as the publicizing of a new 911 emergency number in Colorado Springs (jointly publicized with a Colorado Springs radio station), a series of advertisements publicizing the St. Francis Hospital emergency room facilities (which in 1978 caused a somewhat retaliatory reaction from some county medical society members closely affiliated with a competing hospital), the offering of medical information through a brief radio spot, "To Your Health" (also sponsored jointly with radio station KVOR), and the like. The examples listed above illustrate the use of clear-cut marketing objectives as aids in directing and controlling marketing effort in a health care management setting.

In each of the examples above, cost data were not provided to measure the efficiency of the program. However, the effectiveness goals were clearly stated and met.

In the next section, we will take these programs and explore techniques which could be used to measure the efficiency of the St. Francis marketing efforts.

THE MEASUREMENT OF EFFICIENCY

The "efficiency" concept in health care providers can be expressed in terms of the expenses incurred and the benefits to be received. This input/output relationship requires an understanding of cost behavior. Cost behavior is typically viewed in relationship to a fixed and variable cost concept. Variable costs are assumed to vary directly with some output measurement such as patient days, procedures, exams, or revenue received. Conversely, fixed costs within a relevant range do not vary due to changes in output. The importance of this concept to control of marketing expenditures can be seen in the following manner. If we are able to identify that for each dollar in marketing expenditures we would have X dollars in additional patient revenues, we would have succeeded in making marketing expenditures a variable cost in terms of patient revenues. Therefore, to achieve X dollars in patient revenues we would spend

Y amount on the marketing effort. This can be expressed as $X = f(y)$.

Unfortunately, it is extremely difficult, if not impossible, to define marketing expenditures in this manner. What we do find is that most marketing expenses are fixed costs. We tacitly assume that we will not be able to isolate the increase in patient revenues from our marketing effort. Instead of using patient revenues, it may be desirable to another type of activity output such as visits to the emergency room, occupancy rates of specific beds such as its cancer Pavilion or number of deliveries. Using a non-dollar activity measure also serves to separate the price increases from the changes in volume. I/we were to use the DRG reimbursement rate for the services to be increased, we can convert the revenue requirement into a specific number of services. For example, DRG reimbursement rate for deliveries is $350. If the total additional revenue needed to cover the costs of a program is $35,000, then (35000/350) then 100 new deliveries must be obtained. Is this a feasible number? The decision makers must evaluate this possibility in deciding whether to approve the marketing effort. Because of the difficulty in determining cost behavior and output measurement factors, the budget process becomes the primary control point for the marketing effort. This appeared to be the approach taken by St. Francis. Because control of the marketing effort through the budget process is very subjective, it is important to be as thorough as possible in identifying the key areas to be analyzed.

One type of budgeting technique that stresses detailed information is the zero-base approach. A zero-base process requires the identification of discrete decision packages for each of the marketing activities. The individual responsible for the marketing program would have to define fully the decision package in terms of resources required and to estimate the outputs to be achieved for these expenditures. When this has been accomplished for several levels of funding, the administrator has the necessary information to evaluate the marketing effort. Key areas of the zero-base process include: (1) the amount of resources required; (2) the benefits of approval; (3) the consequences of nonapproval; and (4) the determination of the activity measurement factors. It should be stressed that the input to this form must come from the individual responsible for the marketing activity. Although instructions and guidance can be presented by financial personnel, the actual data must reflect the knowledge and expertise of the individual who will control the effort.

Once the decision packages have been completed, administrators must then rank the decision packages in priority order. If other programs are also under the zero-base concept, then they too would have to be prioritized and ranked. This ranking process provides information to the hospital decision makers as to what the individual managers feel is important, but also allows top management to make tradeoffs among competing programs during final approval.[1]

A sample completed ZBB request is attached as Exhibit One. The completion of the marketing decision package in the detail shown can be the first start in identifying the data needed for measuring the meeting of the efficiency ''goal'' and evaluating the effectiveness of the marketing effort in reaching desired objectives.

A COST/REVENUE MODELLING APPROACH

Efficiency primarily relates to an input/output relationship. For the input requirement several types of marketing expenditures can be identified. The first type usually fall into the start-up and development area. This would consist of the expenditures associated with the hiring of the marketing person or the training of an existing staff member. It would also include the search for and review of available material, such as a series of radio announcements on preventive health care or the development of a program stressing a new service. These types of costs would almost always be considered fixed costs and monitored accordingly. Once the program has been started, continuing expenses would fall into the category of operating expenses.

It is in this area that a separation of the expenditures into fixed or variable cost components would be most useful. For example, let us assume that a program to increase the use of an outpatient clinic was to be started. After the initial development costs have been funded, then the continuing program would consist of operating cost such as the cost per radio announcement as variable costs (VC) and the direct overhead costs as fixed costs (FC). A cost model could be developed which expresses the input relationships for the marketing program in the following manner, as illustrated in Figure 1.

Once the program has been started, it may be run in such a manner that the only incremental costs for continuing the program for

---

[1]For more information on the ZBB process, see ZERO BASE BUDGETING FOR HEALTH CARE INSTITUTIONS, Ray D. Dillon, Aspen, 1979.

Exhibit One

80%   100%   120%
(MINIMUM)   (DESIRED AMOUNT)   (SPECIAL EFFORT)

Package Name __Quality Plus Program__   Department __Administrative__

Management Review Level __Executive Council__   (Organization Level)

Prepared By __Jean Cooper__   Approved By __Kirk Wilcox__

Purpose of Activity:

To provide improved daily service to patients by offering an incentive to employees and to provide a money back guarantee to patients who are unsatisfied with the daily service and/or employees.

Description of Activity:

The program will offer a money back guarantee to patients who are not satisfied with the service they receive from the employees of the hospital. It does not include medical treatment. $10,000 will be deposited in a bank account to pay for claims under this guarantee. At the end of one year, the amount remaining in the account will be used to pay bonuses to the employees involved in the providing of daily service. 10 full-page ads will be placed in the local newspaper stressing this guarantee.

Resources Required:

Personnel	30% of one FTE as part
(FTE)	time program monitor
Salary	$10,000
Fringe	2,000
Equipment	100
Supplies	50
Travel	100
Other:	
Payment Fund:	10,000
Newspaper Ads:	5,000
Total $	$37,250

Activity Measurements

Effectiveness:

A reduction in the current complaint rate from 2% to 1% of admissions

Efficiency:

80% of the amount placed in the fund will be available for employee bonuses at the end of the year.

Benefits of Approval:

(1) Positive reaction by patients.
(2) Positive community reaction to the advertisements.
(3) Competitive advantage over two major competitive hospitals as measured by public opinion.
(4) Employee involvement in the program through increased awareness of patient needs and the possibility of increased bonuses.
(5) Hospital perceived as major innovator in community in upgrading patient services.

Consequences of Nonapproval:

Complaint rate to continue at 2% with resulting decline in competitive position or status quo at best.

Incremental Packages:	Resources Required & Output Achieved
1.	
2.	
3.	

Ranking By Preparing Mgt. Level:	Ranking by Reviewing Mgt. Level:
No. __1__ OF __4__ Packages	No.____ of ____ Packages

the budget period are the variable costs of $500 per TV announcement. It would appear that this type of information is vital for effective decision making. An incremental cost concept is based on the technique of considering only those costs that change from one deci-

Figure 1

Given:

Direct Overhead Costs (FC)	$10,000
Cost Per TV Announcement (VC)	$ 500
Number of TV Announcements	10

Therefore total costs of this program would be

$$TC = TFC + TVC$$
$$\$15,000 = \$10,000 + 10 \, (\$500)$$

Average cost per TV announcement would be

$$\frac{TC}{\text{no. of announcements}} \quad \text{or} \quad \frac{\$15,000}{10} \quad \text{or} \quad \$1,500$$

sion to another, rather than the average cost approach which is prevalent in the health care industry. Average costs have the tendency to distort the decision in favor of additional volume in order to reduce per unit costs. This behavior is explained in greater detail in the next section.

So far, we have concentrated only on the cost side of the marketing question. Although this is important, it is also clear that we do not expend revenues on marketing programs solely to make expenditures. What we do expect is to receive some kind of benefit. For example, in the preceding discussion on a series of TV announcements, Total Fixed Costs of $10,000 and Total Variable Costs of $5,000 (10 announcements times $500 each) were identified. One way in which this information can be used is to ask how much additional revenue each TV announcement must create to cover the cost of the program. Total Incremental Revenue must equal Total Costs for the program to break even; however, a focus on additional revenue per announcement can help to clarify the outputs to be expected. This can be solved by completing the total revenue side of the following equation: Total Revenue (TR) is equal to Total Cost (TC) or TR = TC. Total Revenue can be further identified as the additional revenue (AR) from each announcement times the number of announcements (Q) or AR $\times$ Q = TR. Substituting in the equation TR = TC, we have AR (Q) = TFC + VC (Q). Given the data in the example, we would have:

$$AR \,(10) = \$10,000 + 500 \,(10) \text{ or}$$

$$10 \, AR = \$15,000$$

$$AR = \$1,500$$

Could we realistically expect each of the TV announcements to generate $1,500 in revenue for a total revenue increase of $15,000? The impact of volume becomes quite evident when the program is expressed in the cost model. Assume that we plan on a program with 20 TV announcements. What is the total revenue required to make this program break even? Substituting the new volume in the cost/profit model reveals the following results:

$$AR\ (20) = \$10,000 + \$500\ (20)\ or$$

$$20\ AR = \$20,000$$

$$AR = \$1,000$$

Each TV announcement must now only create an additional $1,000 in new revenue for the program to break even. Although total program costs have increased to $20,000, the average revenue has declined from $1,500 to $1,000. Increasing the volume even more would further reduce the average new revenue needed. The basis to be overoptimistic on volume is evident as it appears to reduce costs. The marketing decision maker must be cautious in interpreting data when there are fixed and variable costs in the program.

For example, the same type of analysis could be extended to the "Express Admission" program. The more cards that are distributed, the less incremental revenue is needed to make the program cost-effective as the fixed costs are spread over more units. In many marketing efforts, the decision to expand or extend should be based on continuing or out-of-pocket costs instead of the full cost data provided by the accounting system to avoid the declining average cost phenomenon.

Familiarity with cost analysis can provide the kind of information to help administrators better evaluate what to expect from marketing expenditures and better estimate if the efficiency goals are realistic. Before the decision is made to start the program, all costs are relevant to the decision if they will not be incurred if the program is not started the same approach should be used for continuing decisions. Only incremented costs should be used in the decision process.

The cost model developed above can also be used to determine what we can afford to pay for individual marketing efforts. For example, let's assume the marketing effort is expected to yield $700 in additional revenues per TV announcement. Substituting the $700 in additional revenues per TV announcement in the equation leads to an estimate of how many TV announcements should be made if the cost information remain the same as in the earlier problem:

$$\$700Q = 10,000 + 500 \ (Q)$$

$$700Q - 500Q = \$10,000$$

$$200Q = \$10,000$$

$$A = 50 \text{ TV announcements}$$

should be made?

The obvious question becomes whether or not the entire program can be expected to generate $35,000 in new revenues, which the $700 increase per TV announcement implies.

The revenue cost model provides a vehicle for estimating the impact of changes in the marketing effort. As illustrated above, it allows the decision maker to make informed judgments about the amount of expenditures that should be made. Even if the cost and revenue data only represent the best "estimate" available, it still serves as a structured approach to evaluate the efficiency of the program. There will be some marketing programs which may not be definitive enough to allow for the use of a cost modelling approach. The budget process will be the primary efficiency tool. However, for those programs for which revenues and costs can be estimated, the modelling approach offers improved information for decision-making.

REIMBURSEMENT CONSIDERATIONS

The objectives of and amounts to be expended for, the marketing program must also be considered in terms of reimbursement policies and the cost-based approach used by many third party payers.

Resources expended for the marketing effort in health care organizations are similar to other indirect expenditure decisions made by management. For example, they could be compared to educational expenses in that they benefit patient care indirectly. They are also similar to administrative expenses such as the accounting department in that the output is difficult to ascertain and measure. How does the hospital receive payment for this type of expenditure? In this respect, marketing expenditures always fall into an indirect overhead classification. Just like any other overhead expenses, they must be allocated through the cost finding process to the patient care department. The cost finding techniques of (1) direct apportionment; (2) step down; and (3) algebraic methods are well known to most health care providers.[2] Because of the legitimate objective to maximize revenues that are received from various payers, the decision on how to classify marketing expenditures will be heavily influenced by the third party reimbursement regulations. However, an effective administrator must also have an information system which reports the marketing expenditures as the direct responsibility of a program or an individual, and some method of measuring the output of the program. Unless these two factors are accomplished the administrator will not be able to control the marketing efforts with any degree of confidence and therefore will be unable to measure the efficiency of the program.

SUMMARY

Realistic marketing objectives are difficult to determine and defining the output in realistic terms is an even more challenging task. However, if adequate management control is to be achieved the administrator and individual responsible for the marketing effort must include determination of these factors during the decision process. The possibility that competitive conditions will require even greater expenditures into marketing efforts can not be discounted. Poorly stated objectives are a common first weak link contributing to the failure of attempts to control marketing efforts. Even with good, clear, well-defined marketing objectives, further obstacles to control are presented by output measurement problems and cost allocation techniques.

Some of the tasks presented in this article can be the first step in better control of the marketing effort. In many programs proper use of the zero base approach in the decision stage can provide the information to develop the cost model for the budget process and evaluation effort. The cost model can then be used to make judgments about the efficiency of the program. In those programs where little output data is available, the budgeting process may be the only tool available. However, the lack of adequate information now should not prevent a continuing effort to develop it in the future.

---

[2]American Hospital Association, COST FINDING AND DATE SETTING, 1968.

SOME REFERENCES

Cooper, Philip D. and William J. Kehoe, "Health Care Marketing: An Idea Whose Time Has Come," PROCEEDINGS OF THE AMERICAN MARKETING ASSOCIATION FALL EDUCATORS CONFERENCE (1978), pp. 369-373.

Gaedeke, Ralph M., Ed., MARKETING IN PRIVATE AND PUBLIC NONPROFIT OR-GANIZATIONS: PERSPECTIVES AND ILLUSTRATIONS, Santa Monica, CA: Goodyear Publishing Company, Inc., 1977.

Kotler, Philip, MARKETING FOR NONPROFIT ORGANIZATIONS, Second Edition, Englewood Cliffs, NJ: Prentice-Hall, Inc., 1982.

Lovelock, Christopher H., "Concepts and Strategies for Health Marketers," HOSPITAL AND HEALTH SERVICES ADMINISTRATION (Fall 1977), pp. 50-62.

_____and Charles B. Weinberg, MARKETING FOR PUBLIC AND NONPROFIT MANAGERS, New York: John Wiley & Sons, 1984.

Miller, John A., "Marketing Basics for Hospital Managers," HOSPITAL FORUM (Volume XXIII, July/August 1980, Number 5), pp. 7, 10-12.

_____and Robin Waller, "Health Care Advertising: Consumer vs. Physician Attitudes," JOURNAL OF ADVERTISING (Volume 8, Number 4, Fall 1979), pp. 20-29 (suggests many additional references).

Montana, Patrick J., Ed., MARKETING IN NONPROFIT ORGANIZATIONS, New York: AMACOM (A division of American Management Association), 1978 (contains many health care marketing applications and articles).

Suver, James and Bruce Neumann, MANAGEMENT ACCOUNTING FOR HEALTH CARE ORGANIZATIONS, Chicago: Hospital Financial Management Association, 1981.

Zaltman, Gerald and Ilan Vertinsky, "Health Service Marketing: A Suggested Model," JOURNAL OF MARKETING (Volume 35, Number 3, July 1971), pp. 19-27.

Family Selection of Long-Term Care Services: It's Not Just the Facility That's Important

Scott M. Smith, Ph.D.

Census records long projected that by the year 2020, the number of elderly Americans will double and by 2030, one of every five people will be at least 65 years old. This phenomenon, caused by the aging post-World War II baby boom group and increased longevity, is expected to jump the number of elderly to 51.4 million, or 17.3% of projected U.S. population. In real numbers, this increase results in 25.9 million additional elderly.

Of particular interest to the long-term care facilities market is the group 85 and older (since this is the time period that health rapidly deteriorates). One federally funded study identified 17% of all elderly as moderately impaired and 23% as severely impaired. It is clear that the severely impaired make up the vast majority of consumers of long-term care services. Many of these consumers are 85 years or older. The 85 and older market segment is important, as evidenced by growth projections estimating an increase from the current one percent of the population to five percent by the year 2050.

In spite of the immediate and longer term projections of market growth, the vision and response of management are best described as limited. Management of long-term care facilities have traditionally focused on day to day operations rather than with market characteristics, changing service needs, or the process by which families

Scott M. Smith is Associate Professor, Graduate School of Management, Brigham Young University, Provo, UT 84602, (801)378-5569.

select long-term care facilities. The purpose of this article is to increase administrator and director understanding of the market's selection of long-term care services and the family decision-making unit responsible for facility selection. Decision maker perceptions of the importance of daily operations and programs are also provided for those directors responsible for the operation of programs and facilities.

GAINING A PERSPECTIVE ON THE SELECTION OF A LONG-TERM CARE FACILITY

Maximizing competitive position within the long-term care market is most often approached by comparing services and features provided by competing facilities. This approach, while fundamentally accurate, ignores the situational context within which consumer decisions are made. The selection and evaluation of a long-term care is unique within the service industry. It is both ongoing and intense for the family members involved. Current experiences and past decisions are continually focused upon by the decision maker because of the "care" or evaluation context within which periodic family visits occur.

Satisfaction with a long-term care facility is contingent upon the urgency of the decision, and financial implications of the decision, the felt obligation to the receiver of services, personal beliefs about consequences of the decision, and the extent of the search and perceived ability to differentiate permanent care options.

METHODOLOGY FOR THE SURVEY

This research is part of a larger study investigating the determinants of satisfaction in the selection of a long-term care facility. All persons surveyed were family, or in some cases friends responsible for the care of those persons currently enrolled in long-term care facilities. The names of those surveyed were obtained by convenience sample of records of 6 long-term care facilities in a major western U.S. metropolitan area. From the 300 persons surveyed, 135 useable responses were obtained. Of these, 124 were evaluated. This further attrition occurred as the result of incomplete or missing information on one or more of the variables included in the analysis.

The response rate of 41.3% was considerably better than expected given that the questionnaire packet included only a cover letter and pre-addressed, stamped envelope for return purposes. The high response rate which occurred without prior notification, reminders, and incentives gives further credence to the highly involving nature of the long-term care decision.

THE RESEARCH APPROACH

The questionnaire items developed identified the relative importance of decision variables used by decision makers in the selection of long-term care services. The process by which the decision variables were evaluated consisted of three stages.

Stage one of the analysis provides an overview of the demographic characteristics of the decision makers.

Stage two of the analysis provides an understanding of the decision-making process (amount of time spent in selecting a long-term care facility, number of facilities considered, and sources of reference used in selecting the facility).

Stage three provides an analysis of decision constraints operating before and after the decision is made, including the situation variables (urgency of the decision, and financial implications of the decision); search and evaluation variables (extent of the search and perceived ability to differentiate permanent care options); personal beliefs about consequences of the decision; and the felt obligation to the receiver of services. This analysis is presented for decision makers identified as being satisfied and dissatisfied with their facility selection decision.

ANALYSIS AND FINDINGS

Stage One: Understanding the Decision Makers

Respondent relationships with the resident are of prime importance in understanding the role of the decision maker. Table 1 shows that 94% of respondents were relatives of the resident, with over 75% of them being members of the immediate nuclear family.

Respondents are characterized as older, with 42% over 65 years of age, and are married or are sole survivors (91%). Concerning ed-

```
------------------------------------------------------------------------
                              TABLE  1

                       RESPONDENT  PROFILE
========================================================================
```

1)	Relationship to Resident		4)	Education	
	Children of resident	54%		Non-High School Graduate	22%
	Parents of resident	12%		High School Graduate	35%
	Spouse	9%		Some College	18%
	Other relative (sibling, grandchildren, other)	19%		College Graduate	14%
				Some Graduate work	11%
	Non-relative	6%			100%
		100%			
			5)	Occupation	
2)	Sex of Respondent			Housewife	31%
				Retired	30%
	Female	66%		Employed	39%
	Male	34%			100%
		100%			
			6)	Total Household Income (1982 dollars)	
3)	Marital Status			Under $10,000 –	32%
	Married	67%		$10,000 – $14,999	15%
	Widow/Widower	24%		$15,000 – $24,999	25%
	Not Married	8%		$25,000 – $34,999	18%
		100%		$35,000 – $49,999	7%
				$50,000 and over	3%
					100%

ucation, respondents are quite well educated with 43% having some college training. Respondents are also characterized as having adequate incomes, though 32% were observed to have incomes under $10,000 per year. This low level of income is largely explained by the large proportion of retired respondents.

Stage Two: Understanding the Decision-Making Process

Respondents indicated that they had little previous experience in making long-term care decisions. When asked if they had previous experience in selection of a facility, 66% indicated no previous experience, 24% indicated some, and 10% indicated a great deal.

The choice of long-term care facilities are frequently influenced by some knowledgeable "other." Respondents indicated that facility choice was most influenced by doctors, family, and facility representatives. Twenty-nine percent of respondents indicated that doctors most influenced their decision of a facility, 21% indicated that family was the greatest influence, and 12% indicated that the facility representative was the most influential. The remaining 38% of the respondents indicated that some other influence was dominant (1% advertising; 9% social worker; 28% misc., other).

Respondents indicated that the selection process was a very short, but intense decision process. Thirty-five percent of respondents indicated that they spent about a week investigating long-term care facilities, while 37% took about a month, and 28% took 6 months or longer.

Regarding the extent of the search process, the average number of facilities visited, called or inquired about through the mail was 3.4. This number was reduced to a smaller number for final consideration, the mean number of which was 1.7.

The analysis of the respondent data showed that the respondent was the primary decision maker, with 46% of respondents indicating that all of the decision was up to them. Twenty-nine percent of the respondents indicated that they made the majority of the decision, and 15% indicated that some of the decision was up to them. The remaining 10%, although now responsible for the resident were not part of the initial facility selection decision.

As would be expected by the nature of the needed care, the resident generally had little to do with the final decision. Only 3% of respondents indicated that the resident had more than a cursory part in the decision.

Stage Three: Understanding the Decision Process

Table 2 shows the dimensions of the decision process, including urgency, financial constraints, obligation, consequences of the decision, and the search and evaluation process. Within the table, two sets of numbers are presented: the percent of all respondents agreeing and strongly agreeing with the statement, and the percent of respondent disagreeing or strongly disagreeing with the statement. The second set of numbers presents the mean scores on the question for the group of respondents satisfied with their long-term care facility. The right hand column presents the mean score for the group of respondents dissatisfied with their long-term care facility.

Results show that respondents were generally believed that a sudden health problem forced them into finding a long-term care facility. This is explained in the urgency and the little time observed in the search process. Most respondents believed that they could not afford long-term care, but could not afford to postpone the care.

Respondents expressed obligation to assure adequate physical, emotional, and mental care. The belief was also strong that these care needs had been met.

Respondents identified as dissatisfied with current care differed from satisfied respondents in three important ways. First, they did not believe that adequate time was spent in evaluating care facilities before making a decision. Interestingly, they also did not believe they were adequately able to assess differences in care facilities. Secondly, they did not believe that serious problems would result if long-term care was not received. Further questions indicated the belief that consequences of making a poor choice would not severely impact on the patient's mental/emotional or physical health. Third, while they did not believe that the mental/emotional, or physical care needs of the resident had been met, they did not profess a high degree of obligation in assuring mental/emotional care. Figure 1 presents a graphic display of the observed attitude means for the satisfied and dissatisfied respondents.

Stage Four: Analysis of Facility Attributes

Figure 2 presents a plot of importance scores observed for 14 facility attributes reported in Table 3. These attributes were evaluated by respondents in the satisfied and dissatisfied groups. It is noteworthy that relative importances placed on each of the facility

TABLE 2

SCALE ITEMS

Item Number	Description of Item	Percent of Responses SA-A% Mean Satis.	D-SD% Mean-Dissat.
A. SITUATIONAL INVOLVEMENT - URGENCY			
1	A sudden health problem lead to immediate action in finding a long-term care facility.	74 1.89	23 2.10
2	At the time of the long-term care decision, I had little time to search for information.	72 2.30	27 2.10
3	There was an urgent need to find long-term care when the decision was made.	92 1.57	8 1.70
4	If long-term care were not obtained, serious health problems would have resulted.	87 1.6	13 2.2*
5	At the time of the long-term care decision, there was an urgent need to obtain care for the resident.	91 1.6	9 1.6
B. SITUATIONAL INVOLVEMENT - FINANCIAL			
1	If nursing home care were not obtained, the costs of health care would have affected our family's financial well being.	62 2.20	37 1.89
2	At the time the long-term care decision was made, I was financially able to afford the care.	29 3.02	71 3.10
3	At the time the long-term care decsision was made, I was financially able to postpone the care.	27 3.00	73 2.89

TABLE 2

(CONTINUED)

Item Number	Item Description	Percent of Responses SA-A	D-SD

C. ENDURING INVOLVEMENT-OBLIGATION

1	I have a high degree of obligation in assuring adequate physical care of the resident.	92 1.54	8 1.80
2	I have a high degree of obligation in assuring adequate mental/emotional care of the resident.	94 1.52	6 2.22*
3	I believe that I have met the physical care obligations.	95 1.67	5 2.10*
4	I believe that I have met the mental/emotional care obligations.	88 1.84	12 2.40*

D. CONSEQUENCES OF DECISION

1	The consequences of making a poor choice would be quite severe to the resident's physical health.	92 1.72	8 2.20*
2	The consequences of making a poor choice would be quite severe to the resident's mental/emotional health.	94 1.67	6 2.00*
3	The consequences of making a poor choice would be quite severe to my personal satisfaction.	99 1.51	1 1.70

E. SEARCH AND EVALUATION OF LONG-TERM CARE FACILITIES

| 1 | I was adequately able to assess differences in the health care that different long-term care facilities provided. | 77 2.03 | 23 2.67* |

```
------------------------------------------------------------------------
                              TABLE 2

                            (CONTINUED)
------------------------------------------------------------------------
Item            Item Description                    Percent of Responses
Number                                              SA-A      D-SD
========================================================================
```

Item Number	Item Description	Percent of Responses	
		SA-A	D-SD
2	I had a preferred long-term care facility before the search began.	42 2.75	58 2.70
3	I found the search for a long-term care facility an unpleasant experience.	67 2.13	33 1.78
4	I spent adequate time in evaluating choices before making a decision.	82 1.97	18 2.44*
5	At the time of the long-term care decision, alternative forms of health care were available.	18 3.26	82 3.10

* Indicates that the differences between groups is statistically significant at the (t<.05) level.

Figure 1

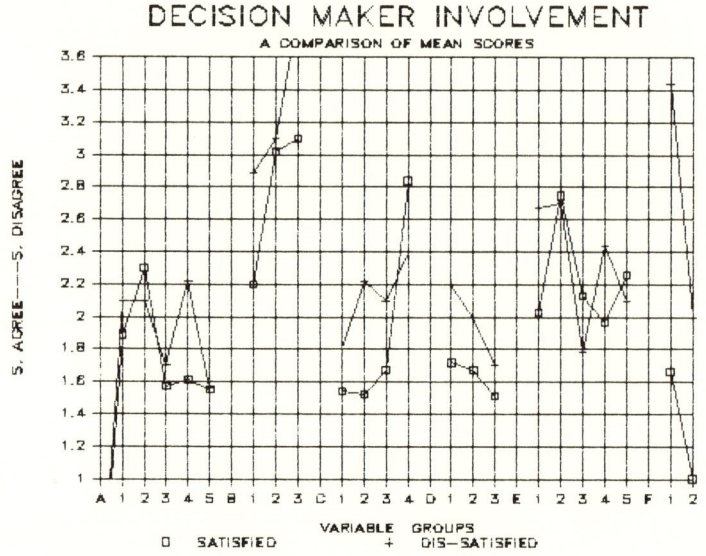

Figure 2

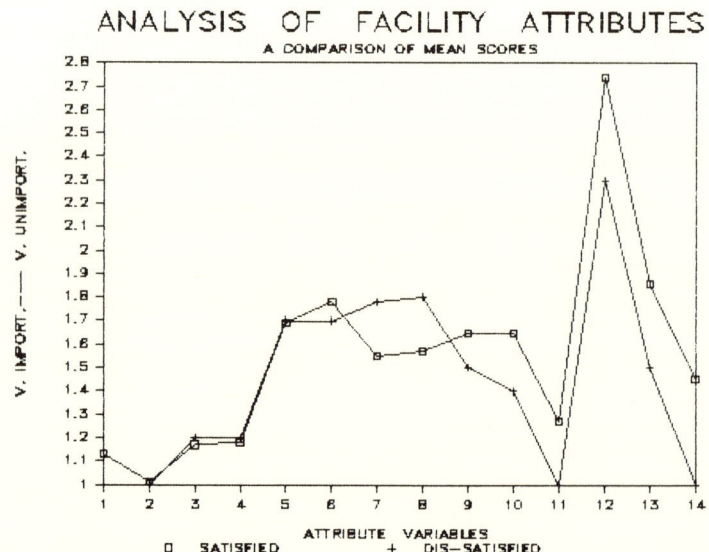

TABLE 3

EVALUATION OF LONG-TERM CARE FACILITY ATTRIBUTES

	Facility Attributes	Mean Importance Score Satisfied - Dissatis.	
1)	Safety of the facilities.	1.13	1.0
2)	Cleanliness of the facilities.	1.10	1.0
3)	Pleasant atmosphere.	1.17	1.20
4)	Courtesy of the staff.	1.18	1.20
5)	Full-time physical therapy program	1.70	1.90
6)	Attractive grounds and building	1.78	1.70
7)	Sufficient building security	1.55	1.78
8)	Daily recreation activities	1.57	1.80
9)	Located close to home	1.65	1.50
10)	Low monthly cost	1.65	1.40
11)	Competent medical staff	1.27	1.20*
12)	Personal phone/tv	2.74	2.30*
13)	Religious observances	1.86	1.50
14)	Pleasant smell	1.45	1.00*

* Indicates that the differences between groups is statistically significant at the (t<.05) level.

attributes is near the same for the two groups. The evaluation of attributes shows that cleanliness of the facility, competency of the medical staff, safety, pleasantness of the atmosphere and courtesy of the staff were of primary importance. Security, recreation activities, location and cost appeared to be of secondary importance. Access to physical therapy programs, attractiveness of the grounds, and the availability of personal phone/tv were the least important attributes to respondents evaluating long-term care facilities.

CONCLUSIONS AND RECOMMENDATIONS FOR MANAGEMENT

The conclusion of this study is that non-facility variables related to the selection of long-term care facilities have considerable impact on management decision-making. Of primary importance is the need for management understanding of the decision process through which decision makers progress.

The first major finding is that the decision process for selection of a long-term care facility is limited in scope and is best described as brief. Respondents strongly indicated that they had very limited time to search for a facility. This time constraint was generally observed to be the function of an "urgent" need for care. This limited search was accentuated by the limited number of facilities evaluated at the time the decision was made. When the typical decision maker begins soliciting information, only about 3.4 facilities were considered. Of these, only 1.7 are seriously considered. Thus, the decision maker's limited size of the evoked set of facilities and short decision time places the decision maker very close to making a decision when contact with representatives of the facility is made.

Secondly, the decision maker knows very little about long-term care facilities. The findings indicate that observable variables, such as cleanliness of the facility, competency of the nursing and medical staff (qualifications of medical and nursing staff), safety, pleasantness of the atmosphere and courtesy of the staff were the most important attributes in the selection decision. Cost of the facilities was not a major point of evaluation. Managerial implications dictate that facility cleanliness and general pleasantness of the staff and administration be kept at a high level, as they are of primary importance in facility selection.

Additional recommendations are derived from the evaluation of the need for communication. Advertising communication directed at decision makers was shown to be of minimal effect. Physicians were reported to have the single largest influence on the choice of a facility. Marketing to physicians as a service to their patients is a promising direction for facility management. Communication is also suggested for the decision maker after the selection decision is made. This communication would assume the role of communicating assurances that adequate care is being administered.

In summary, the traditional management focus on day to day operations rather than with market characteristics, has been shown to be inadequate. As service needs or the process by which families select long-term care facilities changes, management understanding of this process must also expand. It is only through this increased understanding that administrators and directors can effectively interact with the family decision making unit responsible for facility selection.